All Scripture references taken from the KJV of the Holy Bible, unless otherwise indicated.

WHEN NOT HAVING MONEY IS NOT ABOUT MONEY: ***What Could Be Blocking Your Increase***
by Dr. Marlene Miles

Freshwater Press 2026

Freshwaterpress9@gmail.com

ISBN: 978-1-971933-43-6

Paperback Version

Table of Contents

WHEN NOT HAVING MONEY IS NOT ABOUT MONEY:

Did I Miss God? What Could Be Blocking Your Increase

INTRODUCTION

It doesn't take a rocket scientist to realize that if a person doesn't have enough money for things they need for life, then they need to figure out how to get more money. Maybe they need a side hustle, more education, or some other way of receiving more money.

Then that person may look at their budget, because they do have a budget and see that they are earning a sizable income, and they become more confused.

They believe in God. They even go to church and give in the offering, and most of the time cheerfully. They pray, read their Bible, so what is the problem?

So, he then cuts back on his lifestyle, fewer shopping trips, no vacations, no new cars in the past 5 years, no new clothes, but where is the money? Where are the savings? Where are the investments? Why are things so tight?

Next, he will listen to every teaching on Christian finances, read every book and even give seed offerings when provoked in the services.

Still, no change.

Well, there is a change--, things are getting worse. Those seeds have dented the skinny savings account and now it's paycheck to paycheck.

Hey, when I first started coming to his church at least I had some money in savings and I had a little margin in checking. My credit cards are maxed out now because in some services when the pastor calls for the offering, I would be so embarrassed not to put anything in, so I charged it.

You chose carefully. You committed sincerely. You gave when it cost you something. You prayed when it felt repetitive. You stayed when it would have been easier to leave.

You were told that faithfulness would produce increase. You were told that sowing would bring harvest. You were told that perseverance would pay off. So, you sowed again. You gave again. You believed again. Somehow, you are worse off.

The strain is heavier. The margin is thinner. The pressure has not lifted. And quietly, beneath the language of faith, a harder question forms:

Did I miss God?

That question is not rebellion. It is not unbelief. It is not cynicism. It is the question of someone who has tried to obey and cannot reconcile effort with outcome.

This book does not mock that tension. It takes it seriously.

You may never have been told that money might not be the root issue. You may have been taught that more giving solves lack. You may have been encouraged to stay planted no matter what the soil produces. **What soil? Which soil?** We'll get to that.

Scripture begins before money.

Before there was currency, there was weight. Before there was harvest, there was order. Before there was increase, there was alignment. If alignment is fractured, sowing more will not repair it. If structure is unstable, increase will not settle. If something foundational has been missed, more money will not correct it.

This book will not tell you to give another seed, and it will not tell you not to give one either. It will not tell you to wait longer without examination. It will not tell you to abandon discernment in the name of loyalty.

It will ask what governs increase in the first place. It will illuminate many possibilities, so that if something has been overlooked, you will see it clearly.

This is not so you can walk away bitter, it is so you can rebuild in order.

That little talk the pastor gives or that strong teaching the prophet speaks at the special conferences tells me all the same things that are in the books I read, and the lessons I see online, so they must be true, *right*?

They all say: **Give your way out of poverty. Do more. Give more.**

Oddly, I was not in poverty until I started coming to this church and started giving regularly. Instead of increase, I've gotten decrease.

Have I missed God?

I don't like to compare myself to others, but I look around at church, well, starting in the parking lot, most have very nice late model cars, mine is paid for but it is 6 years old. They dress nice, they don't seem to be stressed. Do I dare ask anyone, "Hey how are you doing financially?" No, I couldn't.

They look the part. So, is it only me?

Have I missed God? Really, *have I?*

Maybe I haven't given it enough time. How long does it take for cheerful offerings to multiply? How long does it take for seeds to grow? How long? But it feels like more of a sinkhole than a multi-fold return on what I've sown. And, it's not just this church, this has been happening all of my adult life—everywhere I go, everywhere I sow. I need something to grow and flow to me. *Lord, You know. Please help me.*

YOU HAVE PRAYED

You have prayed. Cried. Lamented. You have given with every possible attitude endeavoring especially to be that cheerful giver. You have smiled with your teeth while your hands have put the last available in the offering basket. You have tried to be faithful.

Still, it seems nothing has moved.

You have heard that giving more will solve it. You have adjusted, corrected, examined your spending, examined your faith. You have examined your motives. You have waited for increase. You have expected stability. Yet the ground beneath you still feels unsettled.

God is Faithful, God is Truth, God cannot lie. These passages have been read to you, so *what's up?* At some point, the question shifts.

Not, "Where is the money?" But it may move to: "Did I miss God?"

That is not a rebellious question. It is an honest one. It is the question of someone who has tried to obey and still does not see what they expected to see. It is the question of someone who does not want to accuse God but quietly wonders whether something structural has been overlooked.

Money answers many things in the visible world. It relieves pressure. It resolves obligations. It creates options. Money is not primary.

When not having money persists, the issue may not be money at all.

Before there was currency, there was weight. Before there was income, there was dominion. Before there was increase, there was alignment. Scripture does not begin with economics. It begins with order. If order is fractured, increase will not stabilize.

If covenant is strained, provision will not settle.

If allegiance is divided, what arrives will not remain.

This book will not offer formulas. It will not give you steps to force an outcome. It will not promise immediate change. What it will do is walk upstream. In this book we will ask what *precedes* increase. It will examine what governs you before anything rests in your hand. The goal of this book is that if something has been missed, you will see it so you can correct the structure, yes to receive. But it is also so that what you receive can remain.

Many people have given and given in the offerings. Many have prayed and prayed, they've believed and believed, and tried to be true. Yet they may be some of the people who are worse off after choosing a church and don't know whether to cut their losses or just hang in there.

They heard the same thing about offerings many times. Now, they may be hoping, Just one more "seed" that oughta do it.

- Sow again.
- Give again.
- Trust again.
- Just one more seed.
- Don’t leave too soon.

These are not rebellious people. But they are tired and possibly confused. They chose. They committed. They leaned in, but somehow they’re worse off.

So you find a sermon that explains that it is the Enemy who is blocking or stealing blessings. How can that be – well, we know he’s not honest, but why don’t I have what I should have based on having sown seed in the offering and given graciously to people, even the guy at the stoplight on the corner? What is going on?

THE OBVIOUS

That same person may be thinking, *I checked everything. What other "things" affect money as much or more than money. Isn't it a no-brainer to look for more money if you don't have enough money?*

So, this book will explore: Is the lack of money linear? Is it simply the lack of enough money? Or, is it a by--product of something else (or other things)? It is mindboggling to think that this is not linear. Income minus expenses equals the amount of money left over. *Right*?

This man is saying, “My expenses are not high at all. It is illogical that I do not have money.”

So, he set out on a prayer vigil and fast with fervent prayers for money. He didn't want to seem greedy or idolatrous, but money is what he needs, so this is what he is praying for, *right*?

God answers prayers while we are yet praying and His answers are, Yes, and Amen.

So, no disrespect, but where is my money? After the fall of man, the ground wouldn't yield easily for Adam, but I am redeemed from the Curse of the Law, so where is my money?

Am I, are people praying for the wrong thing like 90 percent of the time, which is why they don't get what they are asking for. (kinda, what is the real root cause of not having money)

1. Identity & Self-Permission

- Do I believe I am *allowed* to have increase?
- Do I unconsciously associate wealth with corruption?
- Do I sabotage stability because I equate struggle with virtue?
- Was money associated with conflict in childhood?

If someone's internal identity rejects increase, money won't land and it won't stay.

2. Authority & Stewardship

- Does the person manage what they already have well?
- Is there leakage?
- Is there impulsivity?
- Is there avoidance of numbers?

Money responds to stewardship patterns, not prayer intensity or volume.

3. Decision Cycles

Some people don't lack money; they lack timing discipline.

- Starting things and not finishing.
- Quitting jobs impulsively.
- Emotional spending after stress.
- Helping others beyond capacity.

That's not a money problem; That's a pattern problem.

4. Fear & Avoidance

Sometimes lack persists because:

- More money would require visibility.
- More money would require responsibility.
- More money would require confronting skill gaps.

If someone is praying for provision but avoiding growth, that's misalignment.

5. Social & Relational Ecosystems

Money flows through networks.

- Are my relationships healthy?
- Is the person isolated?
- Do they repel collaboration?
- Do they attract users?

Money often follows trust and trustworthiness.

6. Skill & Value Clarity

Money is exchanged for value.

- Does the person know what they offer?
- Can they articulate it?
- Is it structured?
- Is it consistent?

Prayer does not replace competence.

7. Internal Conflict About Desire

If someone prays, "I want financial stability," but internally thinks, that wanting money is carnal or evil, that is doublemindedness; that is internal friction.

What does the pastor or your spiritual leader think about money? That is the Grace you are under.

Where do you work? What is the company's belief about money?

Where do you live? What is the economics like in that area or state? If money is avoiding that whole area and that's where you live, then unless God steps in and makes an exception for you--, there you are.

Money cannot move through contradiction easily.

PRAYING FOR MONEY

Thank God for all those checkpoints, but thank God for this book, because this book is not about any of that. It does suppose that you've checked all that and you've come to realize that something else must be done.

That something else has to be the reason for delays or seeming complete blockages of you receiving money. For example, you have a job and you go to it regularly and work diligently, but you may not be getting ahead. Or, you have a business or maybe more than one, even a side hustle or two. You've established those as channels that God can use to bless you, but what's happening? Where is the increase?

You use Wisdom, you're Godly as much as you can be, you've even prayed about your businesses so they would be sanctioned by the Lord. You're not unethical, crooked, or immoral, so what's the hold up? You do not want money and increase from any source other than the Lord, but times are getting tight and you are resisting desperation at every turn.

So, you pray to God, "Give me money."

Then praying for money alone may be praying at the wrong layer.

Structurally, money is rarely the root variable. It is usually the visible symptom. There are categories that often affect money more than money itself. Perhaps the prayer should be, Lord, show me the leak. Lord:

- Correct my pattern.
- Heal my money trauma.
- Align my stewardship.
- Strengthen my discipline.
- Clarify my value.
- Expose any self-sabotage.

Money may be downstream but if you have not dealt with what is upstream, then downstream you will see different results than desired. That is, no money, little money, lack, frustration. It could be barrenness instead of fruitfulness. It could be delay instead of progress. It could be insufficiency rather than enough.

The real root might be something other than money. So, something other than money could be the reason that a person does not have money. What might those things be? These are the things important to structure: Authority. Identity. Fear. Skill. Ecosystem. Timing. Obedience.

Sometimes lack is not punishment; it's protection. If someone cannot govern $5,000, then $500,000 could crush them. How many people have won jackpots only to be attacked or worse by thieves and other villains? Even in the Bible when two men came from afar, Hezekiah showed them everything in the treasury. The prophet, Isaiah basically asked him why he showed them all that?

In 2 Kings 20 (also Isaiah 39), after Hezekiah recovered from sickness, envoys from Babylon came "from afar." They brought letters and gifts.

Hezekiah did something revealing. He showed them everything--, the silver, the gold, the spices, the precious oil, the armory. He showed all that was found in his treasuries. That's like showing your jewelry that you're wearing, flashing a wad of 100's, showing off your house, art collection, high end electronic devices, and then stepping into the garage to show off your vehicle collection.

Scripture says, "There was nothing in his house, nor in all his dominion, that Hezekiah shewed them not." Nothing was withheld. The prophet Isaiah wanted to know, "Who were these men? From where did they come?"

Hezekiah answers casually. "They came from a far country, from Babylon."

Then Isaiah asks, "What have they seen in your house?"

Hezekiah responds, "They have seen all that is in my house: there is nothing among my treasures that I have not shewed them."

Isaiah says (paraphrased):

> Behold, the days come, that all that *is* in thine house, and that which thy fathers have laid up in store unto this day, shall be carried into Babylon: nothing shall be left, saith the LORD. And of thy sons that shall issue from thee, which thou shalt beget, shall they take away; and they shall be eunuchs in the palace of the king of Babylon. (2 Kings 20:17-18)

In other words, "What you exposed will later be taken." Hezekiah's error was not wealth. It was display. It was misaligned disclosure. It was showing treasure to Babylon.

Babylon did not need to know what was in the treasury. Hezekiah had just experienced a miracle. He had just been healed. He had just had the shadow move backward. He had just received added years. Immediately after that Mercy, he exposed his wealth.

Sometimes lack is not the issue. Sometimes exposure is the issue. So, in God's Mercy, He knows what the unaligned will do. He knows what the ungoverned will do. He knows what a man without discretion will do --, and say. And God also knows what kind of thieves or worse that behavior will draw and whether or not you have the ability to withstand them. So instead of allowing would-be thieves to come and harm you, hurt you, steal from you; He withholds the wealth until you are better situated for such. That is Mercy.

Sometimes increase is delayed because stewardship isn't sealed. Sometimes showing off invites surveillance. Isaiah's prophecy didn't speak of instant punishment; it was about future consequence.

If your current character and structure cannot sustain increase, increase will destroy Peace. As bad as it may feel to not receive, God is showing His Mercy.

By God's Mercy—He may even be protecting your children or your *children's* children. From who? From you. The way you handle yourself especially as it concerns money and wealth, may affect your children and their children if you are not governed. He may be protecting your children and their children from Babylon—the world.

We can celebrate God and give testimony when He blesses us financially, but we don't put it all out there for everyone to see, either by our words, online posting, or beginning to live a showy lifestyle.

In the church, the narrative about money is something like, "ain't got none, give more" and that is so wrong. We all need to pray the right prayer for complete deliverance -- especially when just praying for money over and again may not even be hitting.

WHEN NOT HAVING MONEY IS NOT ABOUT MONEY

It is possible to not have money, but not having money is not the problem.

Else, with all the impoverished people in the world, and even some who are Christians and praying to God, wouldn't God answer them and make them *unbroke*?

A person who does not have money assumes that money is the problem. They may look at all the other aspects of their life, and they decide that if money is not the thing that can fix this, it is certainly the thing that comes the closest to fixing this. No more sleepless nights over bills. A nice house to live in. A dependable or even sporty or luxurious car. I can go shopping when and where and if I like. I can buy things without having to worry about money all the time. They dream of the freedom of having no bills and no bill collectors. They believe they will have no more shame related to poverty, insufficiency or lack. These are blessings to the average man, and they figure money can do all this.

But not having money is not the problem; not having money is a **symptom** of the problem or the problems.

What?

The reasoning appears simple. If there is no money, then money is the issue. If bills press and options narrow, then provision must be the missing piece. The pressure feels measurable. The lack feels visible. The diagnosis seems obvious.

Obvious things are not always foundational things. If money were the root problem, then more money would produce stability. God wants us settled and establish, but He doesn't always just load the asker with money. There's something more to it.

When you ask, you do not receive, because you ask
with wrong motives, that you may spend what you get
on your pleasures. (James 4:3 NIV)

Simple increase would end strain, *right*? Provision would silence frustration. But many have experienced moments of increase without experiencing rest. Some have seen money come and go without understanding why it would not remain. Some have found that money brought them more stress than when they had money. From worrisome family and friends, or sudden haters. No longer being accepted amongst your regular group of friends because of their jealousy, perhaps. Or, trying to jump social levels and not being accepted, bringing on more stress. Others have given faithfully, prayed consistently, adjusted diligently, and still find themselves in the same unsettled place.

When not having money persists despite effort, generosity, and prayer, the question must move deeper.

Before there were currencies, before there were markets, before there were salaries or accounts, two brothers stood before God. They both brought something. Neither arrived empty-handed. One was regarded. One was not.

The difference was not money.

It was weight.

The text is careful in its order. The Lord had regard for Abel and his offering, but for Cain and his offering He had no regard. The person was weighed before the gift. The offering did not secure acceptance. It revealed alignment.

That moment predates economic systems. It predates religious instruction. It predates institutional teaching. And yet it establishes a principle that still governs provision: regard precedes increase.

A person may bring something and still be unregarded. He may labor and still be misaligned. He may approach faithfully and yet remain structurally unsettled.

The absence of money does not automatically mean the absence of favor. But it also does not automatically mean the absence of alignment.

If money were primary, then money would govern stability. But money has never been primary. Dominion is primary. Covenant is primary. Weight is primary. Alignment is primary.

Money responds to those things that are primary.

A person may believe he lacks income, when what he lacks is order. He may believe he lacks opportunity, when what he lacks is disciplined governance over what is already in his hand. He may believe he lacks breakthrough, when what he lacks is restored weight.

The question is not merely, "Why don't I have money?" The deeper question is, "What is being weighed before money ever reaches me?"

This is not a condemnation of desire. Provision is not evil. Stability is not selfish. Increase is not sin. The issue is not whether one desires provision. The issue is whether provision is being treated as primary.

Money cannot create order; it can only rest upon order.

A person who lacks money may be experiencing external hardship, economic injustice, or circumstantial limitation. Such realities are not denied. But where instability persists beyond circumstance, foundation must be examined.

The first recorded rejection in Scripture was not about scarcity. It was about regard.

That should unsettle the simplistic equation that equates money with success and lack with failure. It should also unsettle the assumption that giving alone repairs fracture.

The offering did not fix Cain; his offering exposed Cain. Money functions in the same way. Money does not correct misalignment; it reveals it. It does not repair fractured dominion; it magnifies it. It does not redeem misplaced reliance; it responds to it.

A person may increase his giving and remain unstable. He may multiply his effort and still feel strain. He may pray fervently and yet delay obedience in what has already been made clear.

If what governs him is fractured, what rests in his hand will not remain steady.

When not having money is not about money, it is about structure.

It is about whether scales are honest. It is about whether obedience has been timely. It is about whether covenant has been honored. It is about whether allegiance is singular. It is about whether dominion has been exercised or abdicated.

Money is derivative. It reflects what governs a person. If governance is disciplined, increase stabilizes. If governance is fractured, increase destabilizes. If covenant is intact, provision rests more securely. If allegiance is divided, stability erodes.

A person who treats money as the root will always attempt to solve instability at the visible level. He will adjust income, rearrange expenses, increase offerings, get a side hustle, max out his credit card, or take out a loan to try to negotiate outcomes. But if the foundation is unsettled, what is visible will continue to shift.

Before asking for more, one must ask what is being weighed. Before praying for increase, one must examine alignment. When not having money is not about money, it is most likely about what precedes it.

What precedes it has always been weight.

1. Disorder.

- Chronic disorganization
- No tracking
- No planning
- Emotional spending
- Avoidance of numbers

That's not spiritual attack, That's structural neglect.
Prayers for money won't override disorder.

2. Hidden Pride

- Refusal to start small
- Refusal to take certain work
- Refusal to learn new skills
- *That's beneath me* attitude. Pride can block provision quickly.

3. Fear of Visibility

Money increases responsibility. Responsibility increases exposure. Some people unconsciously avoid increase because increase is so revealing.

4. Misaligned Obedience

If someone is consistently out of alignment in major areas such as: integrity, truthfulness, or follow-through, money instability can be a downstream effect.

5. Vows & Inner Agreements

- "I will never be like my father."
- "Rich people are evil."
- "Money corrupts."
- "I'm not good with money."

Agreements even subtle ones, even forgotten ones, even childhood ones shape outcomes. When someone says something about you, within earshot, even if they say they are joking and you know that is not true, NEVER agree with them and be sure to correct that thing said on the spot. Like what? *Girl, you so crazy.*

Correct it immediately say, "I am not; I am no one's crazy. I am of sound mind and body. I have the Mind of Christ." Sounds small, but it is huge. Untrue statements can accumulate over years and define someone that you are not as who you are. Correct it! If the person won't take correction and continues, consider strongly if you should remain in their presence.

6. Giving as Substitution

Giving can become a substitute for governance. Instead of fixing spending habits. Building skills for life as well as skill handling money. Instead of facing fear, a person gives more and hopes it compensates. That's not faith. That's avoidance dressed as sacrifice.

When lack persists, what governing pattern is operating?

If people are praying, "Lord, give me money," but they are not receiving money, God is not evil. God is not a liar; He cannot lie. God is not broke; everything belongs to Him. Answers to our prayers are Yes, and Amen. So, we keep looking deeper or further upstream to see what conditions may be violated as to why that stream isn't flowing.

We must then consider that there is a reason that money is not flowing to the Christian who prays and I'll say specifically for money. Money should be flowing to that Christian who is a giver, and may even give generously in the offerings because of God's Yes's and Amen's.

Thus saith the Lord, Write ye this man childless, a man that shall not prosper in his days: for no man of his seed shall prosper, (Jeremiah 22:30).

Write this man childless… a man that shall not prosper in his days… That's weight language. That's judgment language. That's structural consequence language. That's not about money first. It's about covenant rupture.

That verse was attached to Jeconiah, a king who broke alignment, broke covenant, destabilized order. The issue wasn't currency. It was authority.

Prosperity was downstream of obedience. Prosperity is not automatic. Prosperity is not mechanical. Prosperity is not transactional. Prosperity is tied to structure.

Jeremiah 22:30 was specific. It was judicial. It was directed. It was not a blanket principle for anxious believers. So, as you are asking, "What could be blocking increase?" be sober and prayerful and ask the Lord if you are under judgment. If He says, "**Yes,**" repent, renounce, and plead for Mercy.

Jeremiah is confirming that what has been written down of the man who prays for prosperity but he is not prosperous. What was written was documentation. It is recorded.

For the man who prays and prays and prays for increase — and yet year after year there is no increase. Pray differently and ask the Lord if parents or ancestors were under judgment. Did they have unpaid spiritual debts? Has any of this fallen on me? Has any of this iniquity been transferred to me? Then repent, renounce, ask the Lord to remove/forgive that iniquity. Plead for Mercy.

At some point, continuing to pray for money isn't about the prayer volume; it may require a man to look to see if there is something written in the spirit concerning him.

It's not that God won't bless, because He will, He does. But, "What has been established that you may know nothing about? What pattern has been set? What structure has been *written*?"

Scripture shows us something sobering: There are moments when Heaven responds with Mercy. There are moments when Heaven responds with instruction. And there are moments when Heaven records consequence.

What if something is written about me? You may ask. What if it has nothing to do with ancestry? What about the patterns that I, myself, have created?

- Chronic broken agreements. Unpaid debts.
- Divided allegiance.
- Delayed obedience.
- Competing hands through wrong or evil alliances.
- Misplaced reliance.
- Seed scattered onto dry ground.

At some point, that becomes a pattern, and patterns produce fruit after their *kind.*

Jeremiah 22:30 did not end the Messianic line. Jeconiah was written childless in terms of reigning authority, yet Christ still came through the lineage. That means judgment did not erase covenant but redirected it.

Something may have been written — but can it be rewritten? Can it be overwritten? Can it be blotted out? Before anything else is written, by choice, habit, or negligence, let's examine the structure.

So, we will say there is something written about a person. This thing written is not known to him, but he is still subject to it.

The tragedy isn't rebellion, it is ignorance of structure. The man is praying. He is sowing. He is hoping. He may even be sincere, but something is *written.* A pattern has formed. An agreement has remained, unchallenged. An alignment has gone unchecked. A foundation was poured crooked and no one told him Yet, he keeps continuing to try to live and build. That's heartbreaking. This person is still subject to what he does not see.

Jeremiah 22:30 is terrifying if it is final. It is redemptive if it is diagnostic. Before anything else is written, let us examine what has already been written by your choices, your agreements, your patterns. What was written about Jeconiah was judicial decree. What is written about many believers today is accumulated consequence.

One is structural fruit. The other is prophetic sentence. Fruit can be uprooted. Patterns can be broken. Agreements can be renounced. Foundations can be rebuilt.

God has not declared you childless.

You may be living under something you do not realize is governing you." What has man said? What your enemy proclaimed either directly against you, or against an ancestor in your bloodline could still be speaking. It should not astound anyone as to the things a spurned lover can say against the one that left them. Yes, there are blind witches and there are witches who know what they are saying.

There are also secret societies and they are occult; that is how they are defined as secret. Who joined up to them? Who got initiated without even knowing it? If someone in your bloodline joined a secret society and dropped off their roles, just stopped going, but didn't get out the right way--, those things could still be affecting a descendant. Unless that descendant is in Christ and has renounced all other headship. But if that person didn't even know they had to do that because they didn't know that their ancestor was a heathen---, well do it anyway, just in case. Do the renunciation.

"Any agreement, covenant, oath, or vow made in my bloodline that was not aligned with God's authority, I do not consent to it. I renounce participation. I withdraw agreement. I align myself solely with Christ. In Jesus' Name, Amen.

I bring these things for your consideration and prayer life. Before you sow again... may we look at something?" You may be that man who is not evil or defiant. You could be serving God to the best of your understanding and ability. By now you may be tired, confused, frustrated. You've been faithful in the ways you were taught, but there is stagnancy in finances.

Let us look at what may already be written. Not written in Heaven as decree but written in habit. Written in alignment. Written in pattern. Written in agreement. Even agreements that were inherited. It may not be you at all. It could be someone in your bloodline that you've never met and could not ever meet as they have preceded you.

Is there an evil covenant made somewhere and you are not aware of it? Therefore, you could not serve that covenant, nor should you want to. Is there a covenant fractured somewhere? Is there divided allegiance? Is there delayed obedience to something you should not even obey?

This could be why some get different results than others in the offering; their foundation is different. You have a better chance of knowing your own foundation than theirs, or trying to appropriate theirs while ignoring yours

CAN YOU CARRY INCREASE?

You've checked with God on judgment. You've done the renunciation; you only belong to Christ and no other idol *gods*.

Now we are getting to you being structured in a way that can carry increase. Jeremiah 22:30 is record. The Blood is erasure of legal hold. What has been written can be blotted out, and that's Mercy.

There are different kinds of *writing*:

1. Judicial decree (as with Jeconiah).
2. Accumulated consequence (as with patterns and alignment).
3. Unexpected, hidden: evil decrees…

The Blood addresses guilt. It cancels legal accusation. It removes condemnation. Evil structure still requires rebuilding. Evil scaffolding erected against you must be torn down.

The Blood blots out the charge. Dominion restores the order. You have authority to break evil covenants in your bloodline. Else, God would not be showing them to you. It is not to torment you; it is so you can, in agreement with Heaven, finally break those bonds and go free. In this way, you can carry increase.

You may ask, *If it's blotted out, why am I still struggling?* The verdict may be erased. But the foundation still needs correction. If a lien is removed from a property, the structure still must be repaired if it was neglected.

Construction. Rebuild. A new altar, a Godly altar, Godly scaffolding in place of what was there before.

Let us see what has been written. Let us see **who** wrote this. When and why may be immaterial, but what has been written and its source will advise you on how you should handle what is either for you, or up against you.

Know this: What has been written can be blotted out but only by the Blood of Jesus.

The praying and paying man who has not yet received should have steady hope, even steadier hope by now. This doesn't mean that everything will turn around tomorrow. There may be layers; he may not just be up against one thing. It could be personal misalignment. It could be a Godly Covenant fracture. It could be an unfilled oath, vow, or promise. It could be spiritual debt. It could be financial ignorance. Unjust leadership, or even territorial pressure. It could be family patterns, economic realities, fear-based decisions, or a combination of several of these or issues like them.

Keep looking." "Seek and you shall find." "Examine yourselves." "Test all things." "Clear the obstacles or blockages, of lack or suffering.

Clear this; clear what the Lord shows you and then proceed on. If you still have another blockage, then endeavor to find out what that is and clear that. Don't hate your ancestors if it is ancestral or familial. Don't hate those who made bad covenants and subjected you to them by not clearing, revoking, renouncing or breaking them themselves, but leaving it to you. Clear what is his to clear. As you clear what is yours to clear, what is not yours will become more visible.

Once internal misalignment is removed, external injustice becomes obvious and then the solution may be movement, not merely more sowing.

Cases of prolonged lack are different because obstacles and blockages are customized. There is no one-size-fits-all. Yes, there are some attacks that are common to man… but the enemy that really wants to limit you, your life, your finances, your ministry, or whatever—, will customize temptations against that man.

This is why you are invited to look and see for yourself; there is not one reason that explains the stuckness of anyone. Were it so, the pastor of your church could preach one message and everyone in the place would be set free. You are unique, but in Christ, you are not alone. You are never alone, in Christ. Amen.

Obstacles are customized. Some are internal. Some are relational. Others may be covenantal. Some are territorial. Some are because of ignorance. Some are misplaced loyalty. Some are simply misalignment or misplacement. Some are inherited patterns. Some are unjust systems. Some are delayed obedience. Some are timing.

For some, maybe even for many-- they are layered.

TEACHABILITY

Can a man who is not teachable… prosper? Can he be aligned? Can he be governed? Helped? Can he be corrected? Can he build anything sustainable?

A man who is not teachable cannot be aligned, not because God refuses him, but because alignment requires correction which requires humility. To be teachable, a person has to be humble.

If a man already **knows (*everything*)**, then he usually closes his mind and cannot be told anything. That man will resent instruction. He will filter everything through ego. He hears but does not adjust, so structure cannot improve. If structure cannot improve, increase cannot settle.

A man can be wounded and defensive and still teachable underneath. A man who is fundamentally unteachable cannot govern. Governance requires feedback.

Kings who cannot receive counsel fall. Hezekiah listened to Isaiah at first. Later, he exposed treasury. That wasn't ignorance, it was lack of guarded Wisdom in that moment. Teachability is not weakness. It is structural flexibility.

Most unteachable men do not know they are unteachable. If they knew, they would already be teachable. Unteachability almost always hides behind something that feels righteous:

- "I have discernment."
- "I already know that."
- "That doesn't apply to me."
- "They don't understand my situation."
- "God told me."
- "I've studied this for years."
- "I've already tried that."

Unteachability rarely feels like arrogance from the inside. On the inside it feels like certainty, or protection. It feels like survival. It feels like woundedness. It may even sound like intelligence. The unteachable man does not experience himself as stubborn. He experiences himself as correct. Unteachability is often invisible to the person because it shows up not as refusal to learn — but as refusal to adjust.

He may listen and seem to hear. He will nod. He will even quote, but he will not change. If a man is praying for increase but cannot receive correction, then he will remain structurally the same.

Structure unchanged means fruit unchanged.

Unteachability is not always arrogance; often it's rigidity that feels like safety. The unteachable man does not wake up and say, "I refuse correction." He says, "I already understand." He says, "Surely there is nothing new to learn." He may say, "That's not my issue." Or, "That doesn't apply to my situation."

He will accept or appear to accept teaching as long as it doesn't require personal adjustment. They may believe that it's for other people. Many times, that will be the person who passes along information that they themselves need but haven't availed themselves to. An unsaved woman was given an evangelistic Christian tract. She gave the tract to her saved sister. *Why*? Because the unsaved sister thought that her saved sister likes Jesus stuff, and she might like to read that. It never registered to the woman who received the tract that what was in it was for her, for her salvation, not for the one already saved.

If obstacles that any man faces are customized--, and they are, then correction must also be customized. The only way to discover what you may be up against, or what is up against you is to always be learning and to remain teachable.

If a man assumes, that he is just like everyone else, he will apply generic solutions. But if he is teachable, he will ask, "What specifically is mine?

What's my fault? What's my problem? How can I solve this?"

A man who is unteachable rarely knows it. Unteachability does not feel like rebellion. It feels like certainty. It feels like experience. It feels like discernment. It even feels like maturity. But it reveals itself in one way: he hears, yet does not adjust. He can quote the instruction. He can analyze the principle. He can even agree with the diagnosis — as long as it applies to someone else.

Increase cannot settle on a structure that refuses correction.

Even a king who cannot receive counsel will see his own house collapse. Unteachability is not the same as ignorance. Ignorance doesn't know. Unteachability won't change.

Some of the most unteachable people are VERY intelligent. Highly intelligent people are often the hardest to teach. An intelligent unteachable person can:

- Rationalize misalignment.
- Theologize resistance.
- Quote Scripture to protect ego.
- Redefine terms to avoid correction.
- Argue structure instead of submitting to it.
- Analyze instead of adjust.

They lean on their own understanding and they make their mind to become a shield or part of a self-proclaimed protective armor. Intelligence increases confidence in interpretation. So, when light shines, instead of pausing, they interpret the light.

Instead of asking, “Is this about me?” they behave as if something came ***at*** them instead of *to* them. They deflect with their mind shield and ask, “Is this doctrinally sound?” They have a tendency to stay in analysis mode, never entering into surrender mode.

Intelligence under authority is powerful. However, intelligence outside authority becomes rigid.

Unteachable spirits often suffer under a form of pride, and for the most part, it is learned. It is intellectual self-reliance. We are taught to lean on our intellect, although the Bible says not to lean on our own understanding. From childhood we are rewarded for:

- Being right
- Having answers
- Solving problems quickly
- Out-arguing
- Being the smartest in the room; getting good grades, gold stars, high marks in school.

Very few environments reward being corrected or sitting in silence. It takes a humble soul to say, “I don’t know.” Most are not rewarded for yielding to instruction. It is considered weakness to revise your position.

Pharaoh could be described as a slow learner, but he never learned at all.

So, the intellect becomes the primary governor.

Not leaning on your own understanding. (Proverbs) does not mean to abandon intellect. It means intellect must not be the final authority. When intellect becomes final authority, teachability dies instantly. At that point, correction feels like humiliation. Humiliation feels like threat.

So, pride protects the mind to protect that person from threat, whether real or simply perceived. If a man governs himself primarily through intellect, then when structure is challenged, he will argue nuance, debate theology, reinterpret terms, shift blame to systems, spiritualize delay, or over-explain patterns, instead of simply asking, "Is this about me?" That's pride.

Intelligence is a gift, but when it becomes the throne, it blocks alignment.

This book is not to shut down intellect, but to dethrone it as something to be worshipped. Ungoverned intellect because it may not be serving you well, if at all.

DOUBLE-MINDED IS INSTABILITY

Unteachability is rigidity, doublemindedness is instability. They look different on the surface, but both break alignment in different ways. A double-minded man wavers, shifts loyalties, hesitates, and starts and stops. He prays one thing, chooses another. Is unstable in all his ways. He leaks. An unteachable man hardens, locks in, and resists correction. Protects certainty. Hears but does not adjust. He calcifies.

Double-mindedness prevents stability. Unteachability prevents correction. A double-minded person can still be teachable. They may waver, but they can receive instruction.

Correction is the gateway to alignment, but the unteachable person cannot be corrected. Of the two, unteachability is more dangerous long-term because it rejects Light, it rejects Truth. Double-mindedness can be stabilized by Light, by Truth.

Double-mindedness says, "I'm torn between two thoughts, between two positions. Unteachability says, "I'm right." One is confused. One is closed. Confusion is curable. Closed is harder. Double-mindedness creates instability in increase. Unteachability prevents increase from ever stabilizing.

If a man is double-minded, he may lose what he gains. If he is unteachable, he may never gain rightly at all. Double-minded people often know they're conflicted. Unteachability rarely knows itself.

The unteachable may likely feel 'stuck' more than the doubleminded. Double-minded feels like **stop and go**. Unteachability feels like **stuck**. A double-minded man tries one direction, then pulls back. He commits, then reconsiders. He believes, then doubts. He moves and then pauses. He experiences motion, but not momentum. His life feels inconsistent. Up and down. Start and stall. Hope and hesitation. That's exhausting. He is not immobile; he is unstable.

The unteachable man stays in the same pattern. He repeats the same explanations. He protects the same structure. This man rejects corrective input and interprets instead of adjusts. He doesn't feel unstable. He feels justified. Externally, he is stationary; that's why he may feel stuck. It's not because nothing is happening, but because nothing is changing.

Double-mindedness is conflict between loyalties. Unteachability is resistance to correction. Double-minded can still say, "I'm not sure." Unteachability says, "I know." So over time, the unteachable man is more likely to experience chronic stuckness.

The double-minded man experiences turbulence. The unteachable man experiences repetition. Repetition without insight feels like fate. A man may be double-minded, but the armored man is more at risk of being unteachable. If someone is unteachable, they may pray fervently, give faithfully, serve consistently, and still never alter the underlying structure; that's the trap.

Ask yourself, "Do you feel unstable, or do you feel stuck?" Those are different problems that require different illumination. The doubleminded man, although he shouldn't expect to receive from God at least has a mind that is open. The double-minded man is conflicted, but he is still moving mentally. He's wrestling. He's oscillating. He's aware of tension.

Unteachability, though… that's quieter and colder. There's no wrestling. There's no tension. There's certainty, which can feel very peaceful from the inside. That's why it's more dangerous.

James 1:8 says the double-minded man is unstable in all his ways. But it is good to know that instability can be interrupted. Conversely, unteachability resists interruption.

The double-minded man may not receive because he wavers, but he still *knows* he's wavering. The unteachable man may feel consistent while remaining structurally unchanged for years. That's the difference between struggle and stagnation. Struggle is alive. Stagnation hardens. The double-minded person can be called to choose. The unteachable person must first be called to see. Choice is easier than sight.

Unteachability is not worse morally. It's worse structurally, because it blocks correction which is the doorway to growth. Unteachability takes deliverance through the Holy Spirit. There may be those who any of us have spent YEARS teaching, sharing, imparting to – so we thought, only to realize much later, they didn't 'get' anything that we were teaching or saying. It's heartbreaking when it's your own child, but we keep praying. Don't lose heart, sometimes that person just needs to hear even what you've been saying from another person that is not you. None of us are called to everyone.

There are people you pour into for years. You teach. You explain. You model. You repeat. You clarify. You pray, then later you realize that nothing shifted. They heard, or believed they heard. They nodded. They even agreed, but nothing restructured.

Some forms of unteachability are not intellectual problems; they are spiritual strongholds.

When pride becomes identity, when self-governance becomes throne, when certainty becomes protection — it is not solved by better explanation. It requires the Holy Spirit. Not louder teaching. Not sharper logic. Not more time invested.

Illumination that pierces armor is not the kind of piercing you can engineer. As an evangelist or teacher, you can inform and water. You cannot awaken. Awakening belongs to God. You can ask for, fast for and pray for awakening, but it ultimately belongs to God.

What soil did the Word fall on?

1. The soil of the person's heart? Sometimes the soil is compacted. Compacted soil doesn't absorb water easily. But compaction can be broken up.

2. **The money strongholds of the family you come from**? That creates a certain *soil* in your heart.

3. The grace of the leader of that place? Does the leader think that poverty is holy? You need to know these kinds of things.

4. Territorial issues of geographic location? That's a larger layer. Geography carries culture. Culture carries norms. But in that moment, territory did not govern the outcome. Authority did.

Not every blockage is territorial. Not every issue is inherited. Sometimes the soil is simply that man's own heart. When truth falls, it does not change territory first. It changes soil, and that determines fruit. Sometimes it takes one moment. One crisis, exposure, loss, or crack in the scaffolding. Then suddenly, what was taught years ago makes sense. It takes the Holy Spirit.

PRAY FOR THE HIGHEST THING

If the devil wants to block you or limit you, he will customize his strategy against you. I personally believe that most obstacles the devil sets are invisible until Light shines. As the saying goes, you will never see what you're looking for if you don't know what you're looking for.

People have a way of believing that they are 'just like everyone else." Nope, that's not true. You may not be a total outlier, but you may not need to be looking for what everyone or anyone else is looking for.

When you were younger, and just beginning to think for yourself and you share something that you think is odd with someone, if they encourage you to pursue it versus, saying, "Oh, that's not true; nothing like that is possible," that could speak to the entire way you see things that may seem improbable. That person may not be right in your case because the things you see are true for you--, that's why God showed them to you or allowed you to see them. Even if they are true for no one else; they are true for you.

Many things are invisible until Light shines. Not because people are foolish. That's not because they're evil, but because familiarity blinds, and because they are taught what is normal, and when to shut up. Some are told to not even think about a thing, so they don't come off as weird.

That is telling someone to shut down their discernment, whether the scolder realizes it or not. They may mean well and want the other person to just "be normal."

People want to fit in. People do not want to *stick out* or be seen as *weird*, so many times they assume that everyone struggles like they do. *Everyone gives like this. Everyone stays like this. Everyone waits like this. Everyone experiences lack like this.* That may not be true at all; everyone is unique. Seek God and seek answers for yourself.

Don't let anyone speak poverty, debt, insufficiency or lack over you and not correct it. Your friend playfully says of the two of you --- two broke girls – **I'm not one of them. Lord, make me the exception. If people are embracing poverty; I reject it, in the Name of Jesus.**

Obstacles are customized. So are callings. So are assignments, and so are alignments. What God is showing you at whatever age you begin to 'see' things, is peculiar to you. It is a blessed person who has spiritually minded people around them who can help them be who they are supposed to be in God. One man's obedience may prosper him. Another man doing the exact same thing may decline.

Why?

Structure. Assignment. Covenant. Placement. Timing. Hidden agreement. You are not worse than everyone else. You are not generic. Blockages are invisible until Light shines, therefore, perhaps your prayer must shift from: "Lord, give me money," to "Lord, shine Light." Light before increase. Some may realize that what is blocking them may not be the devil, but a choice they keep protecting.

The root issue is disorder, fear, identity fracture, pride, skill gap, and emotional instability. Pray for the highest thing; Light is higher than money.

Don't pray for fruit while neglecting the root system. Dear Reader, before you pray for money again, ask these 12 questions. Before you pray for money again, ask yourself:

1. Am I aligned where I am planted? Or am I remaining somewhere God never assigned me?

2. Is there any covenant in my life that is fractured or dishonored? (Marriage, partnership, leadership, agreement.)
3. Am I fully under authority — or selectively obedient?
4. Have I delayed obedience in something clear and concrete?
5. Do I expose what should be governed? (Hezekiah principle — who has access to my treasury?)
6. Is my giving led by God — or driven by fear, pressure, or image?
7. Am I double-minded in my pursuit? (Asking God for increase while relying on something else for security.)
8. Have I mistaken loyalty for assignment?
9. Do I resist correction when it touches something I want to protect?
10. Am I attempting to manage outcomes instead of submitting to structure?
11. Is there misplaced reliance in my life — something I trust more than God?
12. If increase came today, do I have the governance to sustain it?

Now that you've asked those questions, make a decision to pray differently. Instead of praying for the fruit, especially if it is fruit that will be consumed and then it is gone, instead pray for the root. The plant. The foundation. Even the soil. Pray for durable things, higher things. Pray for what will build and last.

HIGHEST THINGS TO PRAY FOR

Instead of praying, “Give me money,” pray for:

1. **Alignment** -“Lord, align me with Your assignment and place me where I am meant to build.”
2. **Covenant Integrity** - “Reveal and repair any covenant in my life that is fractured or dishonored.”
3. **Submission to Right Authority** - “Set me properly under authority and remove selective obedience from me.”
4. **Immediate Obedience** - “Expose where I have delayed obedience and give me courage to act.”
5. **Governance** - “Teach me to guard what You entrust to me.”
6. **Spirit-Led Giving** - “Purify my giving from fear, pressure, or performance.”
7. **Single-Mindedness** - “Unify my loyalties. Remove divided reliance.”
8. **Right Placement** - “Detach me from loyalty that is not assignment.”
9. **Teachability** - “Soften any resistance to correction within me.”
10. **Structural Wisdom** - “Teach me how Your order works before You expand my capacity.”
11. **Proper Reliance** “Remove misplaced trust and anchor my security in You alone.”
12. **Capacity for Increase** “Develop in me the governance to sustain what You desire to give.”

AUTHORITY OVER MONEY

Did the person who is chronically praying for money and not getting any lose the authority to handle money? That is not a financial question, but it does go to the lowest common denominator. This is not about cash flow; this is about capacity; it is a governmental question. This is about character. This is about alignment.

Authority and money are connected because money amplifies whatever governs the person. If authority is intact, then money becomes a tool. If authority is fractured, then money becomes unstable, chaotic, leaking, or absent.

What does it mean to "lose authority" over money? Not that God revoked it randomly, but this could happen if the person abdicated discipline. If they exchanged or surrendered governance to impulse (flesh, sin). If they entered agreement with fear. If they yielded decision-making to emotion. If they violated stewardship principles, or allowed disorder to rule, then the authority over money may have been suspended.

In that state, give in the offerings all you like; those are gifts to the church or wherever you are giving them.

Authority isn't only spiritual; it is exercised in habits. You can't command what you won't govern. In Scripture, authority is often tied to stewardship. He who is faithful in little will become a ruler over much. Authority precedes increase.

If money isn't present or stable, has authority been compromised somewhere upstream? That upstream compromise could look like chronic procrastination. Repeated unfinished projects. Inconsistent obedience. Refusal to confront numbers. Avoiding accountability. Emotional generosity without Wisdom. Spending to self-soothe.

If money is responding to governance, then praying for money while avoiding governance is misdirected prayer. The better prayer might be "Lord, restore my authority." There is:

1. Circumstantial lack (external forces)
2. Structural lack (internal governance issues)
3. Seasonal restraint (Divine timing)
4. Chronic leakage (authority fracture)

1. Scarcity Conditioning - When someone grows up in chronic scarcity, the brain adapts. It shifts to short-term decision making, to immediate relief over long-term planning, risk aversion OR impulsive risk-taking. The thinking pattern becomes present survival focus. This is neurological adaptation, not wickedness. Scarcity changes cognitive bandwidth. That affects money governance.

2. Lack of Financial Literacy – such as not knowing how credit works, how compound interest works, how to track expenses, how to price skills, or how to negotiate. Ignorance is not sin, but it has consequences. Authority requires knowledge.

3. Social Environment - If everyone in your immediate ecosystem is unstable financially, makes reactive decisions, lacks models of wealth-building and normalizes crisis, then dysfunction feels normal. If money authority is rarely modeled, then you may need your authority over money restored. Authority is restored by right alignment with God.

4. Emotional Stress Load - Chronic stress reduces executive function. Executive function governs planning, delayed gratification, critical and strategic thinking, and emotional regulation. When the nervous system is overloaded, governance weakens.

5. Distrust of Systems - Many impoverished communities have experienced institutional betrayal. Many have been excluded from opportunity structures. They have faced discrimination. This creates disengagement from financial systems.

If you don't get involved, you lose your grip on your money. It's not about God punishing you—it's about how the system works, how you think, and the structure around you. Authority isn't just about spiritual power; it's about actually managing things in real life.

If someone has no models, no knowledge, or is conditioned by scarcity, they will not bear increases. If they are overwhelmed by stress, or they are in a dysfunctional ecosystem, they cannot prosper. Their authority over money is impaired.

Poverty is not automatically the result of sin. But patterns of chaos, disorder, impulsivity, avoidance, and abdication can perpetuate poverty.

If someone is praying or constantly praying, "God give me money," but not receiving any money, they may need to pray differently. Perhaps their lack of money is not about money or because of money. What they need is first, regulation of their nervous system. They may need education, discipline, boundary setting or they may need to exit from destructive ecosystems.

You don't pray for fruit when the soil is depleted. You rehabilitate the soil; else the prayer is mis-aimed.

I'm not talking to those who are financially content, but to those who are praying for money because they really need it. The book is especially for those who are praying-but-stuck. The ones who say, "Lord, increase me." "Lord, send provision." "Lord, break lack," but nothing shifts.

Maybe they're praying at the fruit level... while the root is buried. If money is responsive to authority, and authority is in place, then what foundational fractures prevent authority from functioning?

Prayer without alignment becomes repetition. Your prayer for money may not be landing if mis-aimed. Money is not just currency, it is governed by authority, stewardship, order, alignment, discipline and integrity. What ecosystem a person finds himself as well as inner agreements and spiritual covenants will affect how, if, and when money will flow to the one who is praying for increase.

If one of those foundations is cracked, praying for increase may be like pouring water into a broken vessel.

The prayer might need to change because not having money may not be about money. Money is a fruit and there is a whole system that determines what a tree, for example, will bear, in terms of fruit. Perhaps the prayer needs to be deeper, something along the lines of Lord:

- "Restore my governance."
- "Expose my leaks."

- “Heal my fear of responsibility.”
- “Break my agreement with chaos.”
- “Teach me to finish.”
- “Correct my disorder.”

When lack persists beyond season, and prayer remains unanswered, ask whether authority has been compromised.

The lowest common denominator here is authority. Authority over money is exercised in daily patterns. A man needs to be both aligned and governed to maintain his authority. Small slips matter. Small abdications accumulate, such as ignoring bills, avoiding numbers, starting but not finishing, or giving emotionally instead of wisely. Spending to self-soothe and refusing accountability are also small slips of authority.

These don’t seem like dramatic sins; they are governance leaks. Governance leaks cancel authority. You cannot command what you refuse to govern. If someone cannot govern $500, they cannot command $50,000, because authority must be functioning.

Authority is not volume of prayer. The squeaky wheel that gets the oil works in real life, not in matters of spiritual authority. A person could really need money, but without alignment they won’t get it. Authority is alignment with governing principles under God.

If a person is in chronic disorder, in hidden dishonesty, in ongoing compromise, in unrepented patterns (anyone can make a mistake), but this person's authority is compromised. If they are in bitterness, in rebellion against instruction, or refuse to finish what they start, their authority is weakened.

You can be granted authority over finances — and yet abdicate it through your own daily patterns. It could be lost by external forces such as oppression, injustice, war and systemic barriers. There could be structural poverty holding you back where you may lack skill, education or be in a bad ecosystem. Then there is authority fracture—fracture of alignment, obedience and governance patterns.

If someone is praying for provision, but living in spiritual misalignment, their prayer **may not** override their governance structure. That doesn't mean: "God is mad." It means that Authority and increase operate through order.

Because if money amplifies whatever governs the inner life, then God withholding increase could sometimes be protection, not denial. When authority is fractured, increase cannot rest.

IN THE PROCESS OF TIME

Scripture records that Cain brought his offering *"in the process of time."* The phrase appears harmless. It does not sound rebellious. It does not sound defiant. It does not sound dramatic. It sounds patient. Eventual. Reasonable, but it introduces a subtle fracture.

Abel brought of the firstlings of his flock and of their fat portions. Cain brought *in the process of time*. The distinction is not merely agricultural. It is structural. One brought first. The other brought later.

Priority reveals weight. Delay shifts weight.

A person rarely rebels in a single act. More often, he postpones. He moves what should be first into what will be addressed eventually. He convinces himself that the order does not matter so long as the action occurs. Order always matters.

A person may intend to reconcile, but not yet. He may intend to correct imbalance, but not now. He may intend to discipline appetite, but after pressure eases. He may intend to repair covenant, but once conditions improve.

Delay does not feel sinful. It feels practical. It feels like managing complexity. It feels like waiting for the right moment. But when what is first becomes later, weight shifts.

Delayed obedience may interfere with increase. It may restrict what could have rested. It may prohibit what alignment would have sustained. Not because God is vindictive, but because dominion requires order. And order cannot thrive where what should be first has been postponed.

A person who delays what he already knows erodes authority quietly. Each postponed correction trains instability. Each avoided ledger trains disorder. Each deferred conversation weakens structure.

Dominion is not declared. It is demonstrated. It is demonstrated in timeliness. A person who governs what is already entrusted acts promptly when alignment demands it. He does not wait for surplus to repair deficit. He does not postpone integrity until convenience arrives. He does not negotiate obedience based on outcome.

When obedience is moved to *later,* reliance has already shifted.

A person may give generously while delaying discipline. He may sow sacrificially while avoiding reconciliation. He may pray fervently while postponing correction in smaller matters. The visible action appears spiritual. The order beneath it may be misaligned.

Cain's offering was not empty. It was not absent. It was simply not first. And that difference carried weight.

A person who asks why money does not remain must consider timeliness. Has obedience been immediate where it was already clear? Has correction been addressed without delay? Has weight been restored promptly?

Money responds to order. If delay governs, instability follows. Procrastination is rarely labeled rebellion. It does not shout. It does not defy openly. It simply rearranges priority. But rearranged priority reveals allegiance.

A person who postpones what he knows to be right while asking for increase has reversed structure. He has made provision primary and alignment secondary. Alignment precedes provision.

When not having money is not about money, it may be about what has been delayed.

This is not a call to frantic activity. It is a call to disciplined order. Dominion begins in small corrections. It begins in prompt obedience. It begins in honest measurement.

If a person cannot govern what is already in his hand, increase will not repair the fracture. It will magnify it. Before asking for more, he must ask whether what should have been first has been moved to later.

For regard has always preceded provision.

DOMINION BEFORE INCREASE

Dominion is often misunderstood.

It is not volume. It is not visibility. It is not charisma. It is not the ability to command outcomes by declaration. Dominion is disciplined governance over what has already been entrusted.

Before there was money, there was dominion.

A person was instructed to tend, to keep, to cultivate, to name. These are structured verbs that imply attention. They imply measurement. They imply responsibility. They imply completion.

Dominion is not control over others. It is rule within boundary. A person who cannot govern what is within his boundary will struggle to sustain what arrives beyond it. When not having money is not about money, it may be about governance.

A person may ask for increase while neglecting what he already possesses. He may seek expansion while tolerating disorder. He may pray for multiplication while refusing to measure accurately what is already in his hand.

Dominion requires measurement.

False balance is not merely dishonest trade; it is abdicated governance. It is the refusal to weigh accurately. It is the tolerance of imbalance because correction is inconvenient.

A person who does not measure cannot govern. A person who will not confront cannot stabilize. A person who avoids finishing what he begins cannot sustain increase.

Money does not correct this; Money amplifies it. If disorder governs one hundred, disorder will govern one thousand. If appetite governs ten, appetite will govern ten thousand. If avoidance governs small obligations, avoidance will govern larger ones. Disorder does not attract money. Neither avoidance nor appetite doesn't attract or sustain money; all those consume it.

Increase does not create dominion. Dominion creates the capacity for increase. This is not condemnation. It is pattern.

A person may feel that lack of money is restraining him from stability. In reality, lack may be revealing that stability has not yet been built.

Dominion is built quietly. It is built when accounts are faced rather than ignored. It is built when obligations are honored without delay. It is built when appetites are restrained rather than indulged. It is built when what is owed is paid. It is built when commitments are completed.

None of these acts feel dramatic. None feel prophetic. Yet they form the architecture upon which increase can rest. A person who prays for more while neglecting these smaller exercises is asking for amplification without structure.

Dominion is not loud. It is consistent. It is the refusal to let small fractures remain unattended. It is the willingness to correct imbalance immediately. It is disciplined order applied repeatedly. And money, being derivative, responds to order.

A person may believe he lacks provision, when what he lacks is disciplined rule. He may believe he lacks opportunity, when what he lacks is governance. He may believe he lacks breakthrough, when what he lacks is sustained attention to what is already in his hand.

Dominion precedes covenant. It precedes increase. It precedes stability. Without dominion, provision fluctuates. With dominion, provision rests more securely. If a person desires stability, he must first examine governance. What governs him will govern what rests with him.

COVENANT AND THE WEIGHT OF AGREEMENT

Dominion does not operate in isolation. It functions within agreement.

A person does not rule in a vacuum. He lives inside covenants—spoken or implied, written or understood. Every agreement carries weight. Every promise forms structure. Every commitment establishes boundary.

Covenant is architectural language. When a person gives his word, he creates weight. When he enters an agreement, he establishes structure. When he pledges trust, he forms alignment.

If covenant is treated lightly, authority weakens. This is relational order. Trust is the currency behind currency. If trust fractures, exchange destabilizes. If exchange destabilizes, stability erodes. If stability erodes, provision fluctuates.

A person may manage numbers carefully and still breach covenant. He may balance accounts and yet violate agreements. He may speak of increase while quietly dealing loosely with his commitments.

Loose covenant produces unstable outcomes.

A man who negotiates aggressively, shifts terms unfairly, or delays fulfillment of what he promised may believe he is protecting himself. In reality, he is eroding his own structure. Each fractured agreement trains instability. Each broken word reduces weight.

Money does not repair that erosion. Money responds to it. A person may pray for provision while leaving agreements unresolved. He may seek increase while maintaining imbalance in what he has pledged. He may believe that generosity in one area compensates for breach in another.

It does not. Offering does not override covenant fracture. Generosity does not cancel dishonor. Seed does not repair treachery. Covenant must be restored at its root.

This extends beyond formal contracts. It reaches into daily obligations. It reaches into employment agreements. It reaches into spoken commitments that were never written down but were understood.

When wages are withheld unjustly, covenant is breached. When labor is exploited, weight shifts. When what is due is delayed without cause, imbalance is created.

Scripture speaks of withheld wages as something that cries out. That language is not dramatic for effect. It is structural. Injustice produces instability.

A person who withholds more than is right while praying for increase is practicing false balance. He may appear prudent. He may justify negotiation. But imbalance remains imbalance.

Money will not stabilize what injustice has fractured.

This is not to say that every struggling person has exploited someone. It is to say that covenant integrity is inseparable from dominion. And dominion affects what can rest in a person's hand.

Nowhere is covenant more visible than in marriage. Marriage is not merely companionship. It is pledged trust. It is structured promise. It is alignment declared openly.

When covenant in marriage is dishonored—through treachery, duplicity, or sustained disrespect—authority weakens. Trust fractures. Alignment shifts.

A person may compartmentalize this. He may believe that relational breach remains confined to the home. He may increase his giving publicly while neglecting his covenant privately.

But covenant fracture does not remain contained. Authority is not compartmentalized.

A man who dishonors his spouse while praying for increase misunderstands structure. He is attempting to stabilize outcomes while weakening foundation.

Money cannot save a marriage. It cannot restore trust once dishonored. It cannot repair injustice once practiced. It cannot create dominion where discipline is absent. It cannot produce alignment where covenant has been treated lightly.

Money may relieve pressure temporarily. It may create breathing room. But it cannot repair root fracture.

If covenant is unstable, provision becomes unstable.

This is not condemnation. It is cause and effect.

A person who desires stability must examine agreement. Where has word been broken? Where has trust been strained? Where has imbalance been tolerated?

Money will not solve what covenant has damaged. When not having money is not about money, it may be about agreement. Provision rests more securely where covenant is honored.

DOMINION BEFORE WEALTH

In Genesis, God gave dominion long before wealth was discussed.

Dominion means:

- Ordering
- Managing
- Naming
- Cultivating
- Multiplying
- Guarding

Money is simply one modern expression of resource.

If dominion is fractured, resources become unstable. Even if you lack money and want money, the issue isn't, "Do you have money?" The issue is "Are you exercising dominion?" Because stewardship is authority in action.

If someone:

- Avoids looking at numbers
- Refuses to track
- Does not plan
- Makes reactive decisions

• Lets impulses rule
• Won't confront leaks

They are not exercising dominion. And you cannot ask God to multiply what you are not governing. That's structure.

Dominion requires:

1. Order
2. Accountability
3. Delayed gratification
4. Truthfulness
5. Completion

If a person lacks dominion in time management, emotional regulation, boundaries, finishing projects — why would money behave differently?

Money obeys the same internal ruler as everything else. If chaos rules your schedule, chaos will rule your finances. If avoidance rules your emotions, avoidance will rule your money. So, the prayer shifts from, "Lord, give me money." To, "Restore my dominion."

Dominion is practiced. Dominion is quiet. It's balancing books, saying no when you should say no. It is:

• Finishing.
• Planning.
• Tracking.
• Reviewing.

• Adjusting.
• Building margin.

It's not loud; it's disciplined. dominion over money is downstream of dominion over self. If you cannot govern appetite, you cannot govern currency.

If you cannot govern time, you cannot govern income. If you cannot govern speech, you cannot govern contracts. Money simply reveals the condition of dominion.

Some people are born into certain situations, into a certain foundation. Some people are born into fractured foundations. They did not "lose" dominion; they never saw it modeled.

It is not that you sinned, now you're broke. Perhaps you inherited disorder. Inheritance is powerful. If someone is born into financial chaos, no budgeting model.

- Crisis living
  - Emotional spending
  - Distrust of systems
  - No asset-building culture
  - Generational instability

Their foundation is already tilted. Dominion was not demonstrated. It was not taught. It was not normalized. So when they pray, "Lord, give me money." That is not deep enough or right enough. The deeper prayer may need to be, “Lord, teach me dominion.”

There are two broad categories of dominion fracture:

1. Inherited fracture (never taught governance)
2. Chosen abdication (knew better, stopped governing)
3. Demonic or witchcraft attack as a distraction or to throw you out of identity or into survival mode so you are not sitting in your seat of dominion.

Or, the problem could be a blend of those three fracture types.

Foundation determines reflex. If someone grows up in scarcity, their reflex is survival. Dominion requires margin thinking. If someone grows up in chaos, their reflex is reaction. Dominion requires proactive order.

So, the issue may not be “authority lost.” It may be “authority undeveloped.”

Spiritual authority includes dominion over self and resource. Development is progressive. “Before you ask for increase, ask whether your foundation can sustain it.”

NAME IT; GOVERN IT

Once you name a thing, then you can govern it. We must see, understand, and name even these invisible things so we can govern them. Once a thing is named, it comes under dominion.

In Genesis, Adam named everything. Naming implied authority. What was unnamed operated in ambiguity. Look, this could be the invisible structure that has been governing, guarding, or blocking your money. Once named, you will probably recognize your issue instantly.

Before naming there was nebulousness; there was confusion. After naming: clarity comes and there is immediate action. It may not be lack of giving, or lack of faith. It could be a demonic blockage. It could be witchcraft curse. It could just be you, me, any of us needing to repent to the Lord for dealing treacherously with others or in contracts and covenants.

It may be something more subtle. Possibilities:

- Abdicated dominion
- Untrained dominion
- Disordered dominion
- Emotional dominion instead of disciplined dominion
- Spiritual language covering practical chaos
- Sacrifice substituting for stewardship
- Hoping replacing governing

It's got to be something more than, *Give more*. Or, *Budget better*, because we've done all that and none of that has worked.

What if the root is rulership? What if we've abdicated our rightful position of dominion?

Money flows toward order, not because money is spiritual, but because order creates predictability. Predictability builds trust. Trust generates exchange. Exchange generates increase. If chaos rules a life, money cannot sit comfortably there.

Dominion isn't complicated. It's disciplined.

Two more questions to ask yourself: "Have I been praying for increase while avoiding rulership?" Or "I have wanted multiplication without management?"

FALSE BALANCE

Some basics that preacher types don't talk about. Some of those things are found in Scripture: like a false balance.

When did I do that? Maybe you didn't but your dad??? Your grand or great granddad?

A false balance is an abomination. (Proverbs 11:1)

Preachers quote that in business ethics contexts, but where does false balance begin? We assume in cheating scales, dishonest merchants, and corrupt traders. That is certainly where they are found. But what if false balance also means inconsistent weights in personal life?

- Unequal standards
- Self-justification in one area, strictness in another
- Emotional accounting instead of truthful accounting

Inherited measures are real. If a child grows up watching unscrupulous methods such as cash under the table or bills ignored that will be normalized to that person.

- Emotional spending • Tax avoidance
- Generosity used to mask disorder
- Chronic debt as lifestyle

This person may never consciously choose false balance or even recognize it if they did. They saw just that all the time growing up; it is normalized. They inherited skewed scales. Scripture doesn't just condemn false scales. It condemns unjust measures.

Applied spiritually:

Are you weighing obedience lightly?
Are you weighing desire heavily?
Are you weighing discipline lightly?
Are you weighing prayer heavily?

That's false balance; that's false weights. Spiritual authority requires just weights. If someone expects God to multiply, but will not measure honestly, that person is not operating justly. If that person will not look at numbers, that avoidance will cause money to avoid or bypass that person. If he will not will not reconcile accounts or correct imbalance, they are operating with false scales. Wicked if cheating others. Misaligned if cheating yourself.

I am not saying that your father sinned so now you're poor. I am saying, you may have inherited distorted measures. False balance often feels normal. Well, until it's named. Once named, people recognize it immediately. They may even confess, even if silently and within: *"Oh. I justify that. I round that. I ignore that. I excuse that. I delay that."* That's scale language.

Now dominion requires accurate measurement. You cannot govern what you refuse to measure truthfully.

If someone won't:

- Track spending
- Reconcile income
- Confront debt
- Admit impulse

Then they are using uneven weights.

Scripture calls that abominable. Before you ask God to add to your scales, ask whether your scales are honest.

DIVIDED ALLEGIANCE

Covenant fracture is not always open betrayal. Sometimes it is quieter. Sometimes it is divided allegiance. A person may not renounce faith. He may not deny God. He may not openly reject covenant. He may simply anchor himself in two places at once.

Divided allegiance rarely feels rebellious. It feels cautious. It feels strategic. It feels prudent, but it shifts weight.

Scripture presents this tension in subtle figures—men who spoke the language of covenant while clinging to something else for security. They negotiated under the name of God and yet kept hidden idols. They invoked trust and practiced manipulation. They professed reliance while hedging outcomes.

This is not ancient history. It is a pattern.

A person can tithe faithfully and still trust control more than covenant. He can pray for provision and rely more deeply on maneuvering than on obedience. He can speak of faith and quietly anchor his security in something else.

Idolatry is not first about carved images. It is misplaced reliance. It is the transfer of ultimate trust from God to something derivative. It is the belief that what reflects stability can create stability. It is the assumption that what responds to structure can replace structure.

Control can become an idol. Reputation can become an idol. Connections can become an idol. Negotiation can become an idol. Money can become an idol. Money becomes an idol when it is treated as primary. If money is believed to create order, it becomes sovereign in the mind. If money is believed to repair fracture, it becomes redemptive in the imagination. If money is believed to produce alignment, it becomes ultimate.

That is misplaced reliance.

Divided allegiance does not always look dramatic. It often appears in negotiation.

A person may know that reconciliation is required, but he postpones it with a quiet promise: *after I get money*. He may know that correction is necessary, but he delays it until provision arrives. He may know that discipline must be restored, but he negotiates obedience until conditions improve.

After increase, I will fix this. After breakthrough, I will repair that. After provision, I will honor what I postponed. This reverses structure. Alignment does not follow increase. Increase follows alignment.

When a person has obedience conditions on provision, he has already shifted reliance. He believes money will create the capacity for order. He believes income will generate integrity. He believes provision will produce discipline.

But money does not create order. It reflects it. Divided allegiance fractures dominion quietly. It splits weight. It dilutes authority.

A person who anchors himself in God while anchoring himself equally in fear has divided weight. A person who prays for increase while relying primarily on manipulation has divided reliance. A person who gives faithfully while trusting money as ultimate security has misplaced trust.

Money responds to singular weight. When allegiance is divided, stability erodes.

This is not a call to asceticism. It is not a call to reject Wisdom or preparation. It is a call to examine reliance.

What governs the heart governs the hand. If reliance is misplaced, provision will not settle. When not having money is not about money, it may be about divided allegiance.

For money reflects what a person truly trusts.

TREACHERY

This chapter is about the man who seems to be a Believer but he may be doing treachery in covenants, specifically dealing treacherously with his wife. (Equal opportunity here, some women deal treacherously with their husbands.)

Dealing treacherously with the wife of your youth
(Malachi 2:14–16)

That passage is about covenant violation. Treacherous covenant behavior leading to corrupt worship, leads to God rejecting offerings. Of course, we know that rejected offerings do not prosper or bring increase.

This is foundational. You cannot violate covenant and expect clean dominion. Money operates inside covenant. If a man abandons covenant, betrays trust, violates vows, or disrupts household order, he fractures authority at the root. This doesn't mean he will go broke immediately. Many have butchered covenant as they scorch the Earth but somehow they remain financially stable. We must look at how they continue to receive and know that it is not from God. So, I am not talking about that man who is treacherous and violent across the board; he will have his own day of reckoning.

Covenant fracture doesn't stay in marriage; it spreads. Dominion begins and rests in ordered covenant. If covenant is unstable, authority leaks. I am not saying that if you're divorced, you'll be broke although divorce is a divider, not a multiplier. Anyone who has ever been or seen divorce knows that. Poverty is more prevalent in divorced women with children; that is commonly seen.

Treacherous behavior fractures authority. Authority fractured in one domain often weakens authority in others. Scripture links Justice, faithfulness, integrity, weights, and covenant loyalty. If someone deals treacherously with a spouse, with contracts, with words, and with agreements, they weaken the soil in which provision rests.

God doesn't just bless offerings. He examines order. Malachi says, "I will not regard the offering." *Why*? Because covenant was violated. Imagine someone praying, "Lord, increase me, but they are living in covenant breach, relational injustice, hidden dishonor, and exploitative behavior. The issue may not be money; it may be treachery and betrayal of trust.

Trust is the currency behind currency. Money flows where trust lives. Break trust, you fracture exchange. Dominion over money is downstream of covenant integrity. Do not break covenant.

SPOILED COVENANT

When you make covenant with a person that is stronger than you are, you benefit from being in that covenant; their Grace extends to you. When you make covenant with a Person who is richer than you are, then you benefit from their wealth. There are rules related to covenant. Are we keeping them? God lists them in the Bible, and they include not giving corrupt offerings, withholding honor, or using false measures.

Covenant is the container; provision is the content. If the container is cracked, what sits inside becomes unstable. Marriage is one form of covenant. Other forms are contracts, business agreements, words given, promises, and vows made. A person should have handshake integrity. In addition, hidden agreements of the heart should be honored.

If someone spoils covenant regularly, even subtly, they weaken authority. Authority rests on trust; money flows out of that trust. **Money flows on trust.** When a covenant is broken the trust erodes and exchange weakens. This cascade of events leads to destabilization of provision. People may be praying for financial breakthrough while living with **covenant fracture.** If they don't connect the two, they compartmentalize and rationalize saying things like:

> "That's relational."
> "That's spiritual."
> "That's business."
> "That's money."

Scripture doesn't compartmentalize like that. Covenant integrity is foundational dominion. If you betray the wife of your youth, (spouse of any time period of your life) you have demonstrated instability in your highest person-to-person covenant.

If you lie in small agreements, you have demonstrated instability in measurement. If you default on promises casually, you have demonstrated instability in stewardship. That instability weakens authority. Dominion requires consistency.

Money does not sit comfortably in the hands of someone who violates covenant; many times, it completely eludes covenant violators. This is about treachery — deliberate betrayal, dishonor, duplicity.

This book is about covenant. We are graciously invited into and allowed to be in covenant with God.

Covenant is upstream of dominion.

Dominion is upstream of stewardship.

Stewardship is upstream of increase.

So, this is about covenant. Money instability can be a symptom of covenant instability.

All authority flows through covenant alignment, because that second one is larger than money.

RESPECT YOUR COVENANTS

A specialized church accountant came to a church as a guest preacher. His thesis was to the men. He asked them, "How are you treating your wife?" His point was, that God can't or won't do for you what you want if you're not treating your wife well. Then he referenced Kenneth Copeland and Creflo Dollar -- how they honor their wives and pay them for working, giving them the fruits of her labor.

A whole lot of men never learn that. He continued his testimony by sharing that when he first started out in his career as a bookkeeper, his wife helped him all the time even while she had a full-time job outside the home. He states that God instructed him to pay his wife. He complained that he didn't yet earn enough. God won; he ended up paying his wife and after that he began to experience good success in building his fledgling business..

The principle he was pointing to is straight out of Scripture:

So that your prayers may not be hindered.
(1 Peter 3:7)

That verse directly links how a man treats his wife with the effectiveness of his prayers. That doesn't mean that if you forget to take out the trash, God blocks your bank account. It means something more structural.

Marriage is covenant. Covenant is authority structure. If you dishonor covenant, you fracture spiritual alignment. When alignment fractures, authority weakens. When authority weakens, dominion over areas of life—including provision—can be impaired.

That's not prosperity rhetoric. It's governance logic. It's not honor your wife and get rich, it's honor your wife so your prayers will be heard. Covenant honor affects spiritual authority.

Too many still compartmentalize business success from ministry anointing. It would behoove them to put financial increase together with marital treatment. Those are not operating independently. Scripture rarely separates character from consequence.

Now the references to people like Kenneth Copeland and Creflo Dollar were probably meant illustratively — pointing to visible patterns of men publicly honoring their wives. Whether one agrees with those ministries or not, the example was about: Public honor, tangible value, and recognition of labor.

If a man exploits or minimizes the labor of his wife, whether she is helping him in his endeavor or just supporting the household as he presses toward career, he is practicing unjust measurement.

Prayer effectiveness is linked to covenant integrity. God is not simply transactional; He is relational, but authority flows through order. Covenant is one of the highest orders God established. So, even if someone is praying for breakthrough, but violating covenant, the issue isn't money, it's alignment.

This does not mean that every financially struggling man dishonors his wife. Any money blockages you have may be related to something else entirely. This is only presented as an example.

It also does not mean that every wealthy man honors his wife. That would be nice if that were true, but we know it's not. Too many believe or seem to have found a way around the alignment that God requires. They will have to deal with their own choices. We who believe in and serve God want our blessings only from God through Christ Jesus, Amen.

Men who are prosperous certainly doesn't mean that wealth equals righteousness. As asked, how did they get it? But this does mean that covenant dishonor has consequences that extend beyond the relationship itself.

We will keep this in mind, though: Provision may sit inside covenant integrity.

RECONCILED TO YOUR BROTHER

This book is not about giving more to get more. It is also not about budgeting better; that has been

It is about Covenant integrity

- Just weights
- Dominion
- Governance
- Alignment
- Prayer effectiveness

Have you been praying for fruit? Money is fruit, but without the right or no foundation or roots how can any fruit grow? The following verse leads us to another issue of the root that we want our blessings to grow from.

First be reconciled to your brother, and then come and offer your gift. (Matthew 5:23–24)

Go and make up with your brother first, then bring your offering. Jesus does not say, **"Offer first. Reconcile later."** He reverses the religious instinct.

Reconciliation precedes offering.

Why?

Offering without relational integrity is misaligned worship. Malachi speaks about covenant treachery, and rejected offerings. Peter teaches on how prayers are hindered through dishonoring another or others. Proverbs tells us about the abomination of dealing using false balances. Matthew clearly states we are to reconcile before offering.

Scripture keeps tying relational integrity, covenant honor, just measurement, alignment to worship, prayer, and to offering. Of course, offering is directly connected to provision.

Here's the illumination: God is less interested in the gift than who is offering the gift. Recognition: who are you? Who are you to God? Who are you right now? Are you recognizable as a Christian? As a Believer? As a son of God? God is more interested in the order behind the gift, than the gift. God is more interested in you as one of His than what you bring. But what you bring and how you bring it is important, but that should be a true reflection on who you are now and who you are becoming.

God looks on the heart.

If someone:

- Carries unresolved offense
- Violates covenant
- Practices dishonor
- Maintains false weights
- Exploits labor
- Withholds reconciliation …

but still gives and even increases their giving, they are attempting to bypass structure. Scripture keeps saying: Order first. Gift second. People may be praying for financial breakthrough while sitting on relational breaches. They may have never connected those dots.

If a person has compartmentalized Money here, marriage there, brotherhood somewhere else, but elevated what they call prayer to the highest, then the dots will never connect.

Covenant with God is both horizontal and vertical. You cannot destabilize one axis and expect the other to operate cleanly.

TAINTED OFFERINGS

Dominion requires relational order. Relational order means mutual respect as well as observing covenant. Relational order affects spiritual authority. Spiritual authority affects what rests in your hands. That's foundation. You cannot use offerings to compensate for disorder. Offerings do not cover disorder. Especially if the offerings are corrupt, polluted, or improper.

This book is about the architecture of authority. In the Book of Malachi, God speaks of the people bring bad or tainted, imperfect, sick offerings, such as the blemished goat....

> Cursed be the deceiver, who has in his flock a male, and vows it, and yet sacrifices to the Lord what is blemished.
> (Malachi 1:14)

That's not about livestock. That's about substitution. It's about saying, "I will give God this," and then giving Him the inferior version. When you bring God something inferior, not because you had no better, but because you withheld the better, that's covenant dishonor. That's false measure. That's divided integrity.

In Scripture, God keeps saying, I am not moved by ritual when order is broken. A blemished goat today might look like partial obedience. It could look like selective integrity. It could look like tithing faithfully while cheating in business, or being a hellion at home with your spouse and family. It might appear as public giving while living a seriously, unrepented disordered private life. It could sound like sacrificial language with unexamined leaks

Whatever the dollar amount is if the structure is compromised, God will see it. People may be praying for increase while continually offering blemished obedience, then wondering why nothing shifts.

The widow's mite: She gave all she had. Notwithstanding her faithfulness in God, Jesus celebrated her offering. I believe we may infer that her structure was right, so this offering was celebrated. All that she had was not just talk about the amount of the sacrifice, but I believe everything about this widow was in order since Jesus regards who is bringing the sacrifice as well. This widow was looked at for capacity, authority, and character, and it was found that her heart was right toward God, therefore so was her alignment. Else, Jesus would have said other than what He said. (I believe that.)

God's issue in Malachi was not "You didn't bring anything, it was that you brought what cost you least.

Dominion requires full weight.

If you have found yourself or your money problems anywhere in this book so far, you already know what to do. Amen. Adjust your scales where necessary. Adjustment that leads to alignment, which restores authority. Authority stabilizes provision. Restore order so authority can function.

I will not offer burnt offerings to the Lord my God that cost me nothing.
(2 Samuel 24:24)

Now watch how these threads converge. Blemished goat. False balance. Treachery within covenant. Man written down as unprosperous. Unreconciled brother. Hindered prayers. Offering that costs nothing. The issue in each of these cases is not money. These are times when not having money is not about money.

Cost reveals honor. When David refused the free threshing floor, he wasn't being dramatic. He understood something structural: An offering without cost has no surrendered will in it.

Bring the best; it's not like if you were to bring the firstlings of the flock but you decided to bring God… roadkill.

Roadkill is something once alive but found dead on the road, unattended, flattened by traffic and passed over and not in a good way. No, you bring your best; something that cost you something. Spiritually, roadkill is covenant run over by ambition. It is integrity flattened by momentum. It's honor killed by hurry. It's offering made after something vital has already died.

Roadkill. Something found on the way.

Sometimes people are offering what has already been spiritually flattened. They bring a false balance, a blemished goat, or an offering that costs nothing. Pride and unforgiveness may still be raging; there is an unreconciled brother, or anger may be ruling and there is a dishonored wife.

They're giving God what's left after covenant has been neglected. Integrity has been compromised. Justice has been avoided. Reconciliation has been ignored. That's roadkill sacrifice.

It looks religious, but it's already dead. "Lord, forgive me if I have been trying to offer what's already lifeless."

The Holy Spirit in Mercy will bring us under conviction. But the Holy Spirit also brings us into Truth and Truth brings clarity which restores dominion.

Roadkill also implies something else: Movement without awareness. Speed without discernment. Progress that runs over something essential.

How many people chase increase, run over covenant, flatten relationships, ignore weight and measure — and then pray for blessing? That's structural dissonance.

Bringing this into the present: There are at least three modern "offerings that cost nothing":

1. Emotional offerings - Giving what feels good rather than what requires order.
2. Substitution offerings - Giving money instead of correcting behavior.
3. Performative offerings - Public generosity without private governance.

Cost is not always financial.

Sometimes cost is apologizing--, repentance, humbling yourself. Sometimes it is reconciling, admitting dishonor, or correcting false weights. Sometimes it is paying what is owed and closing accounts honestly. Many times, it is simply finishing what was started. Often it is saying NO to impulse and appetite.

All that costs pride; that cost ego, and that may be the deeper sacrifice. Some people are praying for increase while refusing the cost of restored dominion. They want provision without correction. They want multiplication without measurement. They want harvest without soil repair.

That's not greed. It's misalignment. This does not mean: "If you're struggling financially, you must be withholding something. When breakthrough stalls, examine whether your offering has real cost, because cost purifies motive.

Purified motive stabilizes authority. "God does not multiply what you refuse to weigh. You cannot bypass the cost of order with the language of sacrifice.

So, when it's not about money, it could be about honor, Weight, Cost, Alignment, Covenant, and Dominion.

Money is just the visible symptom. Lack of money is the visible pain.

TIMING

Abel brought his offering, but Cain *in the process of time.* (Genesis 4:3–4), brought his.

TIMELY offerings is the lesson here. Disobedience is one thing, but procrastination is rebellion in slow motion.

Abel's offering is described as firstlings, fat portions, first. Abel's offering was intentional. Cain's is described as, *in the process of time.* Not first. Not specified as best. Just something… eventually.

Timeliness is obedience.

Delayed obedience is disorder. Procrastination is rebellion in slow motion. Untimeliness erodes dominion. Dominion requires presence … timely action. When you delay reconciliation, payment, correction, obedience, adjustment, repentance, or discipline, you are allowing erosion.

If someone delays in finances, delays correcting debt, finishing projects, honoring agreements, or even delays bringing their offering to God. Well --. They are practicing slow rebellion against order.

Look at how egregious Cain's delay may have been in bringing an offering. Abel brought the firstborn of his flock, that means he had to wait through gestation (about 5 months). Then care for the animal until the appropriate time (several more months for a proper offering). Abel's offering required months of waiting, tending, and planning-- stewardship.

(Cain's offering). Now it depends on the crop, but typical ranges in the ancient Near East: Barley: ~60 to 90 days. Wheat: ~90 to 120 days. Vegetables: sometimes 30 to 70 days. Produce can be planted and harvested within a season, sometimes much faster than livestock reproduction cycles. Cain could have already brought an offering many times before Abel ever had one sheep to bring. But the text does not suggest that Cain was timely.

Cain's issue was as much about timing and weight as it was about agriculture. He brought something. But not first. Not best. Not weighty.

God respects first and full. He does not reward eventual and partial the same way. That's not prosperity. That's order. Imagine someone praying, "Lord, increase me." while chronically delaying obedience. They lack timeliness, and timeliness is very important to dominion. You cannot govern what you constantly delay.

COMPETING HANDS

Humans may tend to become entangled. With whom? How? Does it matter? How is it affecting receiving increase from God and especially in the offering?

The following is reprinted from the book, **Entanglements: *Illegal Knots Limiting Your Life,*** by this author.

FINANCIAL ENTANGLEMENTS

THE PROBLEM OF COMPETING HANDS

Entanglement occurs when more than one hand begins directing the same area of life. This is especially visible in finances. Competing hands and the cost of shared control could be why some people's money is blocked. Most entanglements do not begin with consent. They begin with assumption. Jurisdiction is often surrendered unknowingly, gradually, politely, in moments of need or convenience. No declaration is made. No agreement is signed. But authority shifts anyway.

Money requires clarity, direction, and singular governance. When multiple hands are involved, progress slows and tension rises. Competing hands look like shared decision-making without clear authority. It can happen in situations where a person accepts financial "help" that comes with influence or control. This can happen when obligations are formed without consent. Pressure disguised as generosity is another pathway. When access is granted during a crisis, but things never get back to normal, or you *never can pay that person back.*

No one may intend to control, but control emerges because jurisdiction that was relinquished, usually for a financial emergency was never reclaimed.

Financial ENTANGLEMENTS may form when a person may accept assistance during hardship. They may defer decisions to keep peace. They may give power of attorney or allow someone else to "handle" finances temporarily. They could prioritize another's comfort over clarity, making ill-advised loans. Those are normal ways, but there are other deeper, darker ways.

You pay money into an altar, even a Godly altar at church. Anything you do with repetition and regularity is "religion." You go to a church, and you put money on that altar, then there is an expectation that you will continue to do that. Any person that you give money to – are they an *altar*? You only need to worry if it is not a Godly altar. If it is an evil altar, it will follow you and try to punish you if you do not continue the worship, no matter what kind of worship it was. Any altar not sanctioned by God is an evil altar.

Families that trade money back and forth all day long create financial entanglements.

At first, this feels like relief, but over time choices narrow, options require permission, movement slows, anxiety increases. Money is not in and of itself evil, as some people believe and have been taught, but the lust for money is where evil comes in. but when authority is divided, Finances cannot move properly. Competing hands is divided governance that can slow money flow to a trickle or cut it off completely.

You ever have a boyfriend (or girlfriend) and money seems a little slow until after you break up with them? Then all of a sudden people who wouldn't help you or give you a dime before are now so generous with you. Yes, you think it's because they didn't like your friend, or because you had a friend and that friend should be helping you. It could be all that, but when we look in the spirit realm, we will see more truth.

Jurisdiction over the money in your hands was unclear. That happens when every decision requires negotiation, when growth creates conflict, when progress feels disloyal, and when independence feels risky. If the person that you are associated with is not self-governed, but instead they are over-governed that affects you in many ways and one of those ways can be your finances.

That is the cost of competing hands. Jurisdictional entanglement: when you've given authority over to people who shouldn't have it, this is competing hands.

If you can say that you did not give up authority on purpose, but maybe you at some time in life allowed it to remain unclaimed, then you are on your way to solving this problem. Unintentional surrender is not failure. It is unexamined access, and once noticed, it can be corrected. This is a good place to look in the spirit and be very prayerful to be sure that you are not entangled in a way that you would not even suspect. Maybe looking at your finances is the first clue. I remind you, it is known on deliverance ground that *spirit spouse* drains **money** from its victims. So you get rid of it and the competing hands issue is abated and your money will flow to you and not away from you again.

GOD DOES NOT BLESS DIVIDED JURISDICTION. God's provision restores **agency**, not dependency.

When finances are entangled obedience is delayed. Generosity is compromised. movement is restrained. God does not advance life where authority is fragmented. Two are not walking together if she wants to tithe and he doesn't. Or, if she wants to give offerings and he wants to go to clubs and drink. How can God bless the money in that marriage? In that house?

Where the people is one, there God commands the blessing.

Life requires direction. Money likes a husband and a wife the most. (sorry singles), but only if that married couple is on one accord. Where more than one hand governs, life slows. *Why*? Because authority is divided. God supplies provision, but He honors jurisdiction.

Many people pray for financial breakthrough when what they actually need is jurisdictional clarity. Money flows best where it is governed. No illegal knot survives once authority is reclaimed.

Money. Order. It will flow.

SPIRITUAL VIOLENCE

Competing Hands can also be God's hand vs. my hand. Whose hand is ruling the resource? Am I governing under authority? Or am I governing independently?

Dominion without submission becomes control. And control fractures alignment. Dominion without submission to God is domineering and it is accomplished by spiritual violence. It is only maintained by spiritual violence.

An offering cannot repair what your other hand is dismantling. Competing Hands about internal division…or about divided loyalty?

Even if a man falls into legalism, like the Pharisees, even tithing on herbs and spices that doesn't mean that God regards that type of offering.

"Tithe of mint and anise and cumin…"
Matthew 23:23

Jesus' rebuke there is surgical. "**You pay tithe of mint and anise and cumin, and have omitted the**

weightier matters of the law: justice, mercy, and faithfulness." God does not regard offerings given that are blemished or from a false balance. Offerings should be real and they should cost the giver something. Obedience should be timely. Furthermore, there should be no other strange hands competing for the increase that God will release because of that offering having been sown.

Legal precision without weight. Legalism is often microscopic obedience in safe areas while neglecting structural obedience in costly areas. They tithed herbs, but they neglected justice. They measured spices, but they ignored Mercy. They counted leaves. All the while violating covenant.

Someone can tithe accurately, give consistently, quote Scriptures on increase, and even pray fervently. They could still be corrupt in other ways such as unjust in contracts. They could be dishonoring in marriage. They might be avoiding reconciliation or practicing false weights. They could be living in disorder, or delaying obedience. These things could hinder their prayers and also the acceptance of their offerings.

A tenth of anise and mint meets legal precision but doesn't address structural neglect. *How ya living?* Jesus calls those "weightier matters." Money is not weightier than justice. Offering is not weightier than covenant.

I am not attacking tithing and neither did Jesus. He said, **"These you ought to have done, without leaving the others undone."** So, I am not saying to stop giving, just don't substitute precision for integrity.

A man can tithe his herbs and still fracture his foundation. Legal obedience in small things does not compensate for disorder in weighty things.

Weight.

- False balance — wrong weights
- Weightier matters — misprioritized weights
- Blemished goat — reduced weight
- Costless offering — no weight
- Cain — delayed weight
- Treachery — broken covenant weight
- Competing hands — divided weight

Weight. Money has weight. Authority has weight. Covenant has weight. Obedience has weight.

Legalism counts ounces.

Dominion measures substance.

HEDGING BETS

Think about Laban in the Book of Genesis. Laban speaks the language of the God of Abraham. He swears by "the God of Nahor." He negotiates. He manipulates wages. He changes terms repeatedly. And he keeps household idols. He operates in covenant proximity —
but with divided loyalty.

That's hedging. One hand in covenant. One hand in control. One hand in faith language. One hand in hidden idols. Now that is extremely relevant today in the times we live in.

Hedging is subtle. It looks like "I trust God… but let me secure myself another way too." "I honor covenant… but let me keep this backup allegiance." Some of these people will be moving in idolatry, New Ageism, and all kinds of other 'religions.' This is not of God, but they either think no one knows or everyone else is doing it.

They rationalize, "I give, but they know they are doing other things too, in order to try to manipulate situations. "I pray… but I do what I must to control outcomes."

Hedging is not atheism; it's double anchoring. Dominion is fractured by double anchoring. It is divided allegiance, and you cannot exercise clean authority with divided allegiance.

A person could pray for provision, but may rely on manipulation. Many speak faith filled words, but operate in fear-based decisions. A person could tithe, but still cheat in small ways--, I'll call it micro-cheating. Many confess trust in God, but maintain backup idols such as items. Also intangible things such as status, control, influence, image, connections.

That's Laban energy. Laban's household looked like constant negotiation, wage manipulation, hidden idols, and instability.

Idolatry is not only bowing to statues; it is misplaced reliance. If someone's real trust is in an image, a system, or a network then God is not the only hand in what they want or expect to receive. When they believe in charm, hustle, control, or emotional leverage, that man can expect to receive nothing from God because that is doublemindedness.

That's hedging, and hedging weakens authority. Dominion requires **singular** allegiance. You cannot rule under God while secretly ruling under fear.

You can't pray for provision while secretly trusting your idol. God does not compete with or cooperate with idols.

Everyone struggling is not an idolater. Where there is divided allegiance, authority is diluted. Diluted authority does not welcome increase.

These are things that may be hindering prayers and increase: false balance, treachery in covenants, untimely obedience – procrastination. Others include unacceptable or blemished sacrifices, legal precision without weight, competing hands, and the subject of this chapter: hedged allegiance

They all point to one thing: Divided integrity. divided integrity weakens dominion. Money simply exposes it. Now I'll ask you something before you rest for real: Is this book about restoring singular allegiance? Because if that's the core, money becomes a diagnostic, not the destination.

MISTREATING EMPLOYEES

Mistreating employees. That is not HR. That is covenant and weight.

He that oppresseth the poor reproacheth his Maker. (Proverbs 14:31)

Behold, the wages of the laborers… which you kept back by fraud, cry out. (James 5:4)

Wages withheld cry out. That means unjust treatment of labor is not invisible or silent.

If someone underpays labor, delays wages, exploits employees, if he extracts without honoring or demands loyalty but gives no fairness, they fracture authority.

Withholding that which leads to poverty is not disciplined saving. It is unjust hoarding. Money responds to justice. Not because money is moral, but because justice stabilizes systems.

Unjust systems eventually destabilize. Destabilization drains wealth. Provision resists injustice. You cannot build increase on exploited ground.

Dominion is stewardship, not exploitation. People may be praying for financial breakthrough, but true increase is tied to responsible management, not ruthless extraction. A steward protects, cultivates, and uplifts those under his care, knowing that every act of injustice undermines the foundation he stands on. Exploitation, on the other hand, is shortsighted; it sacrifices the future for fleeting gain, leaving behind a legacy of broken trust and eroded relationships. Financial prayers may rise, but if stewardship is neglected, the answers will not materialize as hoped.

We can't separate these things saying, *This is business. This is spiritual. This is money. This is worship.* Scripture doesn't separate them. Every transaction, every decision, every relationship is an act of worship or a betrayal thereof. Integrity cannot be segmented; the character that governs business must also govern faith, finances, and devotion. The illusion of separation only masks inconsistency and permits compromise. When we treat money as merely secular, we lose sight of its power to reveal our true priorities and allegiances.

Unjust wages are not just an HR violation but a spiritual indictment. Every withheld dollar, every delayed payment, every undervalued laborer sends ripples through the moral and economic fabric. It is not merely a human offense; it is a reproach to the Creator. Injustice in compensation poisons trust, undermines morale, and invites instability into the enterprise. The cries of the wronged echo beyond the boardroom, reaching the very courts of heaven.

It's the same architecture. Whether in business, church, or home, injustice erodes the structure from within. The blueprint of increase is built on the pillars of fairness, honor, and transparency. Remove these, and the edifice crumbles, no matter how impressive its outward appearance.

Withholding that leads to poverty is not disciplined saving. It is unjust hoarding. Money responds to justice. Not because money is moral, but because justice stabilizes systems. Hoarding breeds scarcity and resentment; it is a denial of provision's true purpose. Wealth flourishes in environments of equity, but shrinks where injustice rules. The flow of resources is intimately tied to the ethical climate—where fairness prevails, prosperity follows; where injustice festers, stagnation and loss are inevitable.

The consequences are not only economic but spiritual. The ground cries out, and the heavens answer. A foundation of exploitation is a curse masquerading as increase; it cannot sustain true abundance. Justice is the only soil in which lasting prosperity grows. To ignore this is to invite ruin, regardless of short-term gains.

HE THAT SCATTERETH

Scattering that increases is not reckless giving. It is just and timely distribution.

There is one who scatters, yet increases more;
And there is one who withholds more than is right, but
it leads to poverty. (Proverbs 11:24)

There is he that withholds more than is right. That's not wise saving. That's unjust withholding.

The issue is not generosity versus thrift; it's justice versus control.

The man who is scattering that which is another man's --- works for the devil.

There is a man who builds, and there is a man who scatters. The difference is not always visible at first. Both may speak confidently. Both may appear discerning. Both may claim standards. Both may even call their behavior "truth." But over time, fruit reveals posture.

A scatterer is not merely someone who disagrees. He is not simply critical. He is not merely opinionated. A scatterer diminishes what he did not build. He tears down reputations casually. He writes words that erode trust. He sows doubt where he has no jurisdiction. He undermines restaurants, businesses, churches, leaders, authors, competitors — sometimes not even to gain advantage, but because erosion is his disposition. He can do all of this by writing scathing and lying reviews online, for example.

He may call it discernment. He may call it honesty. He may call it high standards. But if his wake leaves depletion instead of strengthening, division instead of clarity, instability instead of order, that man is scattering. This behavior, this scattering has consequence. A man eventually lives inside what he rehearses. If he spreads suspicion, he will not be trusted. If he spreads diminishment, he will not be supported. If he spreads erosion, **he** will not be preserved.

Scattering is not just an action; it is a pattern. Patterns form atmosphere. You cannot practice erosion and expect preservation. You cannot diminish others and expect multiplication. You cannot scatter and expect gathering. Structure does not allow it.

You may say, "What does this have to do with money?"

Everything.

If you ask for increase while practicing scattering, you are asking for what your character cannot sustain. Increase requires stewardship. Stewardship requires governance. Governance requires alignment. A scatterer lacks governance. The daily protection of alignment is governance.

If a man cannot or will not guard another man's work, how will he guard his own? If he cannot speak carefully about what he did not build, how will he preserve what he is given?

The issue is not competition. Healthy competition builds excellence. Scattering tears down to compensate for insecurity. The scatterer is often fear-driven. Fear says there is not enough. Appetite says take from another. Pride says expose them. Comparison says diminish them.

But the Spirit says build. The works of the Spirit Build. The opposite of scattering is building. The works of the Spirit gather and preserve. Faithfulness guards what is entrusted. Gentleness refuses casual destruction. Self-control restrains appetite. Patience rejects urgency. Kindness strengthens rather than erodes. Peace stabilizes atmospheres. Love refuses to compete destructively.

The Spirit builds; the flesh consumes. The man governed by the Spirit strengthens environments. The man governed by appetite weakens them. One gathers. The other scatters.

This is written as warning. Eventually a man's character settles onto his own life. He may rise quickly. He may gain traction. He may feel momentum. If his pattern is erosion, he will eventually inhabit instability. Character determines sustainability. And sustainability determines increase.

If you desire increase, ask yourself honestly:

- Do I build more than I diminish?
- Do I strengthen what I touch?
- Do I guard what was entrusted to me?
- Or do I rehearse scattering?

This is not about perfection; it is about posture. Alignment produces governance. Governance produces preservation. Preservation allows increase to follow. Scattering disrupts all of it. Increase does not follow erosion.

A man who lives by judgment will eventually live under it. A man who habitually judges others harshly eventually finds himself measured by the same standard. Judgment rehearsed becomes judgment inhabited. The measure a man uses does not remain external. Over time, it becomes the measure applied to him. Structure will return to you what you rehearse.

NEW CLOTHES

I've heard more than one guy say something about throwing out old stuff to make room for the new.... is that in the Bible? then I won't worry about that kind of stuff. There is no Scripture that says, that a person should throw out your old stuff so God can send new stuff. That's modern motivational language.

What IS in Scripture is give no thought as to what you will wear. And, this:

No one puts new wine into old wineskins. (Matthew 9:17)

That's about spiritual capacity and covenant transition — not decluttering your closet to attract blessing. It's about structure being able to hold what is coming.

Put off the old man… put on the new. (Ephesians 4:22–24)

That's about character transformation, not spring cleaning for breakthrough. It's more like Israel clearing leaven before Passover. (Exodus 12). We are looking at symbolic purification, more than furniture management. The idea that if you don't throw out old clothes, God can't send increase, is not Biblical. That's superstition wrapped in spiritual tone.

Provision is not blocked by stored boxes. God is not waiting for garage space.

Decluttering can lead to psychological clarity, order restoration, removing distraction, practicing dominion. But it is not a spiritual law that triggers money. Throwing out items does not activate covenant.

However, if someone holds onto things out of fear, scarcity mindset, or emotional attachment that signals distrust. that's an internal issue, not a closet issue. The problem would be the fear. Not the object. You don't need to throw away old shoes to receive provision; you need to drop the fear.

You need just weights, covenant integrity. That man needs timely obedience, undivided allegiance. He needs Justice and true stewardship. God requires alignment; He's not looking for space in your closet, else there'd be a husband's wardrobe in there by now.

IN NAME ONLY

Dry Christians put themselves at disadvantage when it comes to receiving from God, even if their prayers are sincere and the results are deeply needed. Prayers, only when you want something doesn't work with God any more than in the natural only calling on friends or family for needs and favors.

Prayers for the same thing over and again. Prayers for yourself and not others. No worship, no exalting God to His place on the throne of your heart. In church every Sunday, or at least Christmas, Mother's Day and Easter but for lip service or for real?

Oh God when You bless me then I'll serve You.

Relationship with God, like those with people, requires genuine connection and ongoing engagement—not merely reaching out when you need something. Christians who approach God only during times of crisis or need, without investing in worship, gratitude, or regular communication, may find themselves spiritually "dry" and unable to fully receive the blessings or guidance they seek. Just as friendships grow through consistent interaction and mutual support, so too does one's spiritual life deepen through regular prayer, worship, and honoring God, not just when asking for favors. When faith is reduced to a transactional exchange—praying only when you want something—it lacks the depth and sincerity that foster true spiritual growth and receptivity.

The tendency to pray repetitively only for personal needs without considering others or truly worshiping God is a pattern that reflects a shallow spiritual practice. **Authority cannot be self-centered and transactional** rather than relational. Attending church out of habit or tradition, rather than sincere devotion, is likened to giving "lip service." The heart of faith is not found in ritual attendance or mechanical prayers but in authentic worship, exalting God, and allowing Him to be central in one's life. True spiritual vitality involves caring for others in prayer, genuine worship, and a consistent relationship with God that goes beyond special occasions or emergencies.

The statement, *"Oh God when You bless me then I'll serve You,"* illustrates a conditional approach to faith—promising devotion only after receiving blessings. This attitude misses the essence of true faith, which calls for unconditional worship and service regardless of circumstances. God is not a vending machine dispensing blessings in exchange for promises. Instead, spiritual maturity is demonstrated through consistent service, worship, and alignment with God's will, independent of whether one's needs are met. Serving God should stem from love and reverence, not as a bargaining chip for personal gain.

In summary, the selected text challenges believers to move beyond surface-level faith and transactional prayers. It calls for a deeper, more authentic relationship with God—one marked by consistent worship, selfless prayer, and genuine devotion, not just requests in times of need or ritual participation. This kind of spiritual engagement opens the heart to receive from God in ways that mere requests cannot.

ABIDING

Keeping your mind stayed on Jesus, but not just His name.

As people pray, 'in the Name of Jesus'.... they just say the name, call the name.... But in the character of Jesus, if we know and abide there that is far different than just saying the name. There is a difference between saying His name and abiding in His nature.

In the name of Jesus is not a verbal stamp or a punctuation mark. In Scripture, name represents character, authority, reputation, nature, alignment.

To pray "in His name" is not to append syllables. It is to pray from within His character. That changes everything. A man can say the name of Jesus while still operating in fear, appetite, pride, competition or other works of the flesh. That man may be actively scattering. He may be a transactional man.

To abide in His character means humility governs you. Truth governs you. Mercy governs you. Righteousness governs you. Alignment governs you.

Keeping your mind stayed on Jesus is orientation. It is thinking like Him. Valuing what He values. Refusing what He refuses. Moving at His pace. Operating under His order. That's abiding.

You cannot pray "in His name" for increase while refusing His character in governance.

The authority in His name flows from alignment with His nature. That's why the sons of Sceva failed. They used the name without alignment. Authority cannot be borrowed without surrender.

Jesus' Name is not a password. It is a posture. It is a lifestyle. To pray in His name while resisting His character is to separate authority from alignment.

This is about knowing Christ and loving Him. It is about affection, and affection changes everything. Imitation can be manufactured. Affection cannot. You can mimic tone. You can borrow language. You can rehearse posture, but you cannot fake Love.

Keeping your mind stayed on Jesus is not mental discipline alone, it is relational orientation. It is affection that steadies thought. When affection is real, you don't have to force surrender. You don't have to perform alignment. You don't have to strive for authority. You remain.

Remaining produces likeness naturally. That's not "fake it until you make it." That's, abide and it forms you.

Affection quiets fear. Affection restrains appetite. Affection stabilizes governance. Love displaces anxiety because fear is quieted by Love, Power, and a sound mind.

Perfect love casts out fear.

So, if a man is praying "in the name of Jesus" but has no affection for Him— his prayer is transactional. If he abides in affection, alignment follows without strain, and that's why authority feels easy. Love makes surrender light.

His name is not a formula to activate results. It is the expression of a relationship. Intimacy and true *agape* Love may be what any person is lacking. They may not be missing money at all, but affection.

Many humans can tell you about many make-believe characters, mostly from childhood stories, but what do they know about Jesus? Perhaps it is because fairytales were told over and over, but stories about Jesus -- maybe not so much. My point? Do people really realize that Jesus is **real**?

Children can recite the lore of kings, superheroes, wizards, villains, and even entire fictional universes. They know origin stories, motivations, powers, and turning points. Because those stories were told repeatedly and vividly. With imagination. With affection.

But what do they know of Jesus? Let it not be only a few flannel-board scenes. A cross. A resurrection line. A moral summary.

But He is a Person.

If a child hears about dragons fifty times, but hears about Christ twice, which one feels real? Repetition builds reality in the imagination. Affection builds attachment.

If Jesus is only presented as a doctrine, a rule, a moral teacher, a distant Savior, or a Sunday topic, then He becomes abstract. To be loved deeply, Jesus has to be much more than an abstract reference. I need to put down the childish stories and learn what I can about the Person, Jesus of Nazareth, the Christ of God.

> When I was a child, I spake as a child, I understood as a child, I thought as a child: but when I became a man, I put away childish things. (1 Corinthians 13:11)

When Jesus is presented as living, present. active, personal, authoritative, and real, then affection forms. Affection sustains alignment. Jesus is real so surrender is relational. Jesus is real so "in His name" is not incantation; it is alignment with Someone.

Because He is real, fear diminishes. Appetite settles. Scattering becomes unthinkable. Alignment becomes natural. Affection follows reality.

Because Jesus is real, money cannot be ultimate. Because Jesus is real, increase is derivative. Because Jesus is real, governance is relational.

If Jesus is not real to a person, then money becomes more tangible; humans are prone to cling to what feels tangible.

Jesus is real, so governance is not theory; it is obedience to Someone. He is real so surrender is not discipline; it is response. Jesus is real so "in His name" is not phrasing; it is alignment with living authority.

If Jesus is not experientially real to someone, money will feel **more real.** Pressure will feel **more real.** Bills will feel more real. Fear will feel more real.

Humans orient toward what feels tangible.

If Christ is only conceptual, but money is concrete, guess what governs?

So, the question is not, Do you know *about* Him? It is, *Do you know Him*? Affection forms toward presence, not concepts.

We must then keep our minds stayed on Jesus.

Jesus is real, so the mind does not stay on a word--, the name, Jesus. It rests on a Person. Affection toward that Person grows from interaction.

Money feels real because it is visible. Pressure feels real because it is immediate. But Christ is not less real because He is unseen. He is more.

Jesus becomes real to a man. So now where that man now places fear will change. Fear loses its dominance, it's authority.

Fear thrives in perceived aloneness. When Christ is abstract, a man feels alone under pressure. When Christ is real, that man is no longer alone in it. Once fear loosens, appetite changes, urgency calms. Comparison quiets, and scattering feels unnecessary.

Peace under pressure becomes possible. When Christ becomes real, fear no longer has the loudest voice. It may still speak, but it does not govern. Governance returns when fear is dethroned. When governance returns, alignment becomes natural.

When alignment leads, increase follows.

MONEY IS DERIVATIVE

Money is not primary; it never has been.

It did not exist when the first offering was weighed. It did not govern when dominion was assigned. It did not create covenant, nor did it establish trust. It has always functioned downstream.

Money is derivative.

It reflects what precedes it.

Provision does not create order. It rests upon it. Stability is not produced by increase. It reveals whether increase can remain. Income does not generate alignment. It exposes whether alignment already exists.

A person who treats money as primary will always attempt to repair instability at the visible level. He will increase revenue, adjust spending, multiply giving, negotiate opportunity, and seek breakthrough. But if what governs him is fractured, what rests in his hand will not remain steady.

Money amplifies structure. If discipline governs, increase stabilizes. If avoidance governs, increase destabilizes. If covenant is intact, provision rests more securely. If allegiance is divided, stability erodes.

Money is not sovereign. It is responsive, behaving downstream according to what is upstream of it. Because it is responsive, it must not be worshipped. To worship money is to treat derivative power as ultimate power. It is to believe that what reflects structure can replace structure. It is to assume that what responds to order can create order.

It cannot.

A person should not lean on things that are changeable. Money is changeable. (no pun). So who is in charge of money? The world's systems will fail, the Bible tells us that. History proves that. Empires collapse. Currencies devalue. Institutions rot. Policies reverse.

Markets shift. Currencies fluctuate. Governments rise and fall. Systems collapse. Industries evaporate. If you lean your stability on something that moves, you will move with it. This is not spiritual drama, this is common sense.

Money flows within systems. But systems are not sovereign. So, who is in charge of money? Not banks or governments, or markets.

If a man's peace is anchored to systems, his peace is fragile. But if his heart is anchored to Christ who does not fluctuate, then money becomes a tool, an instrument, not a throne. That is the place and position for money.

God governs provision. Provision and money are not identical. Provision can come through systems. But it is not limited to them and that's why leaning on money is dangerous. Money is unstable.

Jesus is the same yesterday, today, and forever.

Alignment must lead. Authority must govern. Increase must follow. If money leads, fear returns.

Christ is real, so fear loses grip. When fear loosens, money loses its emotional authority.

Systems fail; God never will. God cannot fail. Ever.

Money cannot save a marriage. It cannot restore trust once dishonored. It cannot repair injustice once practiced. It cannot create dominion where discipline is absent. It cannot produce alignment where covenant has been treated lightly.

It may relieve pressure temporarily. It may ease strain for a season. But it cannot repair fracture at the root.

A person who believes money will repair what covenant has damaged has misunderstood structure. A person who believes income will generate integrity has reversed order. A person who believes provision will produce discipline has mistaken symptom for source.

Money reveals. It reveals honest scales. It reveals delayed obedience. It reveals divided reliance. It reveals fractured covenant.

If instability persists, it may not be because provision is absent. It may be because structure is unsettled. There are times when a person believes he is being denied increase, when in reality he is being protected from amplification. Increase magnifies what is present. If disorder governs, disorder will multiply. If appetite governs, appetite will expand. If covenant is fractured, pressure will intensify. If dominion is weak, instability will increase with volume.

In such cases, withheld increase may not be rejection. It may be restraint. Protective, not punitive restraint.

A parent does not hand greater responsibility to one who has not yet learned governance. Not because love is absent, but because weight without structure creates collapse.

Provision operates similarly. This does not mean every season of lack is protective. External injustice exists. Economic systems fail. Circumstances constrain. But where instability persists beyond circumstance, a person must ask whether structure can sustain what he is asking to receive.

Increase is not only about obtaining more. It is about sustaining more.

Sustainability requires dominion. It requires covenant integrity. It requires singular allegiance. It requires honest measurement. It requires timely obedience.

Money follows what governs a man. If what governs him is fractured, money will expose it. When not having money is not about money, it is about what precedes money.

And what precedes money has always been weight.

Follow the money? Is that wise, since money, itself is already a *follower*?

ASSIGNED GROUND

Provision is not tied only to effort. It is tied to alignment which includes placement. A person may exercise dominion faithfully and still labor in ground that was never assigned to him. He may work diligently in an environment shaped by entrenched disorder. He may give generously in a system that resists justice. He may govern responsibly in soil that cannot sustain what he builds.

Hard work does not override misplacement.

Scripture does not ignore geography. It does not treat ground as irrelevant. It ties promise to movement. Abraham was instructed to leave familiar territory. Not because his homeland lacked soil, but because assignment and ground were linked.

Placement matters.

A seed planted in unsuitable soil will struggle regardless of its integrity. The problem is not the seed. The problem is the ground.

A person may be sincere, disciplined, covenant-keeping, and yet positioned in an environment that resists increase. Collective injustice exists. Corrupt systems exist. Entrenched dysfunction exists. Environments can reinforce instability and punish integrity.

Scripture recognizes principalities and patterns over regions. It recognizes exile. It recognizes displacement. It recognizes that environments shape outcomes, but placement is not an excuse.

A person cannot attribute every instability to atmosphere while ignoring internal order. Internal fracture does not become external destiny. Dominion must be examined before territory is blamed. Dominion is examined, placement must also be considered.

A man may be out of alignment geographically. He may be clinging to familiarity rather than obedience. He may be anchored in comfort rather than assignment. He may be positioned where his structure cannot bear fruit. Effort in the wrong place produces exhaustion rather than stability.

Some remain in environments that continually erode what they build. They work, recover, rebuild, and repeat the cycle. The instability is not solely internal. It is reinforced by surroundings that normalize disorder.

A person must ask: Is this ground assigned? Or merely convenient? Assignment carries Grace. Misplacement carries friction.

Abraham's provision was tied to movement. Israel's stability was tied to covenant alignment on specific ground. Exile for them was not merely political displacement; it was separation from structured promise.

When not having money is not about money, it may involve placement. It may involve location. Are you where you are supposed to be? Living? Working? Going to and giving in church? Are you where God has assigned the blessings for you?

A person who has restored weight, corrected covenant, disciplined dominion, and aligned allegiance may still need to examine **ground**. If structure is sound and instability persists, placement deserves sober evaluation.

Increase cannot settle where assignment is resisted. This is not a call to impulsive relocation, but be sure to discern or ask whether the ground you are on aligns with calling.

Provision follows alignment. Alignment includes place. Money is derivative. It reflects not only internal structure, but whether internal structure is planted in suitable ground.

When ground and governance align, stability becomes more attainable and more sustainable. When ground resists governance, effort becomes strain.

A person who desires increase must consider not only what governs him, but where he stands, where he sits, and where he lives. He must remain in his God-appointed jurisdiction.

MONEY ANSWERETH ALL THINGS

There is a verse that unsettles every argument made so far. It appears blunt. Final. Almost absolute.

Money answereth all things.

A person reading these pages may think: If money answers all things, then how can it be derivative? If money answers all things, then how can it not be primary?

The verse is real. It is not to be ignored. But what does it mean? It does not say money creates all things. It does not say money governs all things. It does not say money redeems all things. It says money answers.

An answer is a response. Money responds to need. It responds to demand. It responds to transaction. It responds to exchange.

Money answers within a system. It answers bills. It answers contracts. It answers obligations. It answers material demands. Within the visible order of earthly exchange, money functions as a practical responder. a responder is not a ruler.

Money answers questions within the material realm. It does not answer questions of alignment. It does not answer covenant fracture. It does not answer dishonor. It does not answer misplaced reliance. It does not answer dominion erosion.

Money may resolve an invoice. It cannot resolve treachery. Money may secure a house. It cannot secure trust. Money may purchase comfort. It cannot produce stability. Money may create access. It cannot create alignment.

The verse does not elevate money to sovereignty. It acknowledges its functional power within earthly systems.

A hammer answers the problem of a nail. That does not make the hammer sovereign over architecture. Money answers many practical problems. That does not make it foundational.

If money answered all things absolutely, the wealthy would be the most stable, the most aligned, the most at peace. They are not. Money answers in its realm. It does not answer in the realm that governs it.

Money answers the visible. Structure governs the visible.

The verse does not contradict structure. It clarifies function.

Money answers what it was designed to answer. It was never designed to answer weight.

When not having money is not about money, it is because the question being asked is deeper than transaction. Money may answer the symptom. It cannot answer the structure.

if structure remains fractured, the answers money provides will be temporary.

Money is a responder. Alignment is foundational.

PRAY HIGHER

A person who does not have money will naturally pray for money. There is no shame in that impulse. Provision matters. Stability matters. Relief matters. The pressure is real.

But when not having money is not about money, prayer must move upstream. If money is derivative, then asking for money alone addresses the surface.

A child may desire a reward. There is nothing wrong with that desire. But reward follows formation. A sweet may follow achievement. The child may pray for the reward, but he must first learn his letters. Literacy precedes sweetness.

So, it is with provision.

A person may pray for increase. But if weight is fractured, increase will not remain. If covenant is breached, provision will not settle. If dominion is undisciplined, stability will fluctuate. If allegiance is divided, what arrives will not endure. If placement is misaligned, effort will strain.

Prayer must rise higher than the symptom. It's not simply, "Give me money," but "Restore my scales." It's not "Send provision," but "Correct my weight."

Not "Break lack," but "Establish dominion." Not "Increase my income," but "Align my covenant." Not "Open doors," but "Place me where I am assigned." This is not the denial of provision. It is the reordering of it.

A person who continues to treat money as primary will continue to pray at the wrong level. Misdiagnosis produces repeated frustration. The cycle continues: pray, give, wait, strain, repeat.

But when prayer shifts to foundation, structure changes.

Ask for honest measurement. Ask for timely obedience. Ask for courage to reconcile. Ask for discipline in small governance. Ask for singular allegiance. Ask for rightful placement. Ask for the highest thing. For when the highest thing is restored, what reflects it begins to respond.

Money is not sovereign. It never was.

It answers in its realm, but it does not govern the realm that produces it.

Provision follows structure. Stability follows alignment. Increase follows dominion. If foundation is repaired, the prayer for money changes. In some cases, it becomes unnecessary in the way it once was. Provision begins to respond to order.

Continue to treat money as ultimate, and it will continue to frustrate you. Restore what governs you, and what rests in your hand will follow in its measure.

Pray higher.

AMEN.

I seal these words decrees, declarations and prayers across every dimension and timeline, past, present, and future, to infinity, in the Name of Jesus.

I seal them with the Blood of Jesus and the Holy Spirit of Promise.

Any retaliation against this author, the reader or anyone who prays these prayers, makes these decrees and declarations at any time, let that retaliation backfire on the head of the perpetrator to infinity, and without Mercy, in the Name of Jesus.

Dear Reader

Thank you for acquiring this book and supporting this ministry. I pray this book has accomplished what it set out to do--, break any obstacles that keep you from receiving increase from God. It will take some diligence, but you can be successful.

Shalom,

Dr. Marlene Miles

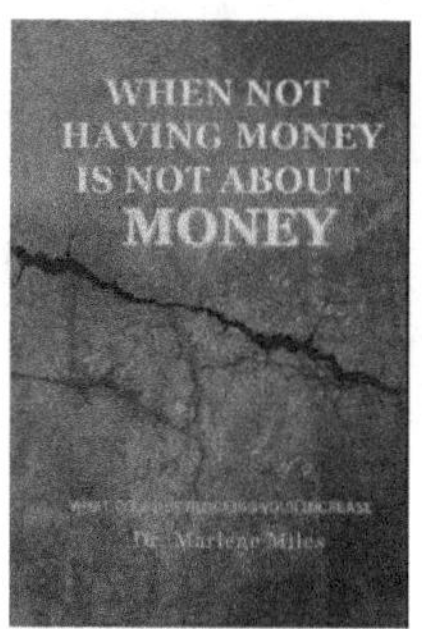

New Releases:

Christ of God (*The*) 3-book series

Christ of God, (*The*) Box Set, includes all 3 books

Prayerbooks by this author

There are some books that are only prayers. You just open up the book and pray.

FAKE FRIENDS: *Prayers Against Betrayers*

HOLIDAY WARFARE Prayer Manual (humorous) Surviving Family Gatherings All Year Long (without catching a case)

SOUL TIE Prayer Manual (The) Part of a 3-part series including a workbook.

MAD at DADDY Prayer Manual – part of a 3-part series including a workbook.

Healing the Sibling & Relative Wound Prayer Manual

Healing the Father-Son Wound Prayer Manual

Prayers Against Barrenness: *For Success in Business and Life*

Breaking Curses of the Mother Prayer Manual

Prayers Against Barrenness: *For Success in Business and Life*

Fruit of the Womb: *Prayers Against Barrenness*

Beauty Curses, *Warfare Prayers Against*
https://a.co/d/5Xlc20M

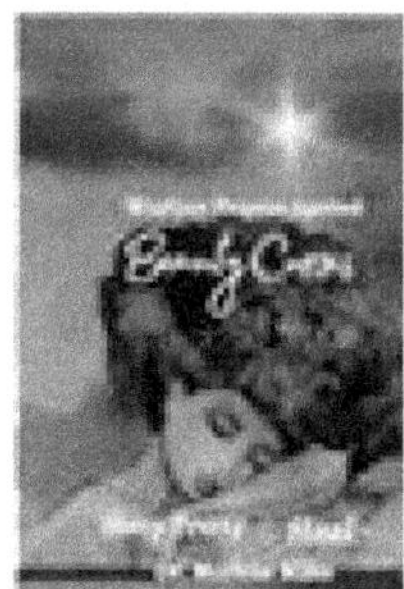

Courts of Marriage: Prayers for Marriage in the Courts of Heaven *(prayerbook)* https://a.co/d/cNAdgAq

Courtroom Warfare @ Midnight *(prayerbook)* https://a.co/d/5fc7Qdp

Demonic Cobwebs *(prayerbook)* https://a.co/d/fp9Oa2H

Every Evil Bird https://a.co/d/hF1kh1O

Gates of Thanksgiving

Spirits of Death, Hell & the Grave, Pass Over Me and My House

Throne of Grace: Courtroom Prayer

Warfare Prayer Against Poverty https://a.co/d/bZ61lYu

Other books by this author

Abundance of Jesus (The) https://a.co/d/5gHJVed

AK: The Adventures of the Agape Kid

Already Married in the Spirit: *Why You May Not Be Married in the Natural*

AMONG SOME THIEVES https://a.co/d/dkYT4ZV

Ancestral Powers

Anti-Karen: *How To Mind Your Own Business Without Minding Other People's*

Anti-Marriage, *The Spirit of*

Backstabbers https://a.co/d/gi8iBxf

Barrenness, *Prayers Against* https://a.co/d/feUltIs

Battlefield of Marriage, *The*

Beware of the Dog: Prayers Against Dogs in the Dream.

Bless Your Food: *Let the Dining Table be Undefiled* *https://a.co/d/6oPMRDv*

Blindsided: *Has the Old Man Bewitched You?* https://a.co/d/5O2fLLR

Break Free from Collective Captivity

Broken Spirits & Dry Bones

By Means of a Whorish Father

Caged Life: Get Out Alive! https://a.co/d/bwPbksX

Casting Down Imaginations

Christ of God (*The*) 3-book series

Christ of God, (*The*) Box Set, includes all 3 books

Churchzilla, The Wanna-Be, Supposed-to-be Bride of Christ https://a.co/d/eAf5j3x

Collateral Damage: *When What Happened Spiritually Was Your Fault*

Deep Poverty: Get Out of Poverty and Its Shame

Demonic Cobwebs (prayerbook)

Demonic Time Bombs

Demons Hate Questions

Devil Loves Trauma, *The*

Devil Weapons: Unforgiveness, Bitterness,...

The Devourers: Thieves of Darkness 2

Do Not Swear by the Moon

Don't Refuse Me, Lord (4 book series)

https://a.co/d/idP34LG

Dream Defilement

The Emptiers: *Thieves of Darkness, 1*
https://a.co/d/5I4n5mc

Entanglements:

Evil Touch

Failed Assignment

Fantasy Spirit Spouse https://a.co/d/hW7oYbX

FAT Demons (The): *Breaking Demonic Curses*
https://a.co/d/4kP8wV1

The Fold (5-book series)

- The Fold (Book 1)
- Name Your Seed (Book 2)
- The Poor Attitudes of Money (3)
- Do Not Orphan Your Seed (4)
- For the Sake of the Gospel (5)
- My Sowing Journal

Gang Ups: Touch Not God's Anointed

Gathered: No Longer Scattered
https://a.co/d/1i5DPIX

Getting Rid of Evil Spiritual Food

https://a.co/d/i2L3WYQ

got HEALING? Verses for Life

got LOVE? Verses for Life https://a.co/d/8seXHPd

got HOPE? Verses for Life

got money? https://a.co/d/g2av41N

Has My Soul Been Sold? https://a.co/d/dyB8hhA

Here Come the Horns: *Skilled to Destroy* https://a.co/d/cZiNnkP

Hidden Sins: Hidden Iniquity

https://a.co/d/4Mth0wa

How to Dental Assist

How to Dental Assist2: Be Productive, Not Wasteful

How To Stay Prayed Up

How to STOP Being a Blind Witch or Warlock

I Take It Back

In Multiplying I Will Multiply Thee

Into Freedom:

Irresistible: Jesus' Triumphal Entry
https://a.co/d/d09IfEC

KNOW YOUR BATTLE: Stop Swinging Blindly — and Win Against Opponents, Adversaries & Enemies (Workbook) https://a.co/d/eOwFKlV

Legacy

Let Me Have A Dollar's Worth https://a.co/d/h8F8XgE

Level the Playing Field

Living for the NOW of God https://a.co/d/6bK5duE

Lose My Location https://a.co/d/crD6mV9

Love Breaks Your Heart

Mad At Daddy: Healing Father-Wounds that Affect Motherhood (book, workbook & prayer manual)

Made Perfect In Love

Mammon https://a.co/d/29yhMG7

Man Safari, *The*

Marriage Ed.: *Rules of Engagement & Marriage*

Made Perfect in Love

Money Hunters: Beware of Those

Money on the Altar https://a.co/d/4EqJ2Nr

Mulberry Tree, *The* https://a.co/d/9nR9rRb

Motherboard (The)- *Soul Prosperity Series*

Name Your Seed

Occupy: *Until I Return* https://a.co/d/bZ7ztUy

One Defining Day*: A Day When Dreams Come True*

Opponent, Adversary, or Enemy?: Fight The Right Battle with the Right Weapons

https://a.co/d/byQqEE2 & companion workbook: Know Your Battle

Plantation Souls

Players Gonna Play

Portals: Shut the Front Door: Prayers to Close Evil Portals.

Power Money: Nine Times the Tithe

https://a.co/d/gRt41gy

The Power to Get Wealth https://a.co/d/e4ub4Ov

Powers Above

The Robe, Part 1, The Lessons of Joseph

The Robe, Part II, The Lessons of Joseph

Seasons of Grief

Seasons of Siege: God Is Coming

Seasons of Waiting

Seasons of War

Second Marriage, Third--, *Any Marriage*

https://a.co/d/6m6GN4N

Seducing Spirits: Idolatry & Whoredoms

https://a.co/d/4Jq4WEs

Shut the Front Door: *Prayers to Close Portals*
https://a.co/d/cH4TWJj

Siege: *God Is Coming*

Sift You Like Wheat

Six Men Short: What Has Happened to all the Men?

SLAVE

Sleep Afflictions & Really Bad Dreams
https://a.co/d/f8sDmgv

Soul Prosperity soul prosperity series 3

https://a.co/d/5p8YvCN

Soul Ties: How Soul Ties Form, and How To Break Them (book, workbook & prayer manual)

Souls In Captivity

The Spirit of Anti-Marriage

The Spirit of Poverty https://a.co/d/abV2o2e

Spiritual Thieves https://a.co/d/eqPPz33

StarStruck- Triangular Power series.

SUNBLOCK- Triangular Power series.

The Swallowers: *Thieves of Darkness*, 3

Take It Back

This Is NOT That: How to Keep Demons from Coming at You

Time Is of the Essence

Too Many Wives: *Why You Have Lady Problems*

Tormenting Spirits https://a.co/d/dAogEJf

Toxic Souls

Triangular Power *(series)*, Powers Above, SUNBLOCK, Do Not Swear by the Moon, TARSTRUCK

TRIBE: *What Covenants Are Governing You…?*

Unbreak My Heart: *Don't Let Me Die*

Uncontested Doom

Ungovered Hunger: How Unchecked Appetite Dismantles Authority

Unguarded Hours, *The*

Unseen Life, *The* (forthcoming)

Upgrade: How to Get Out of Survival Mode Toxic Souls (Book 2 of series) , Legacy (Book 3 of series)

The Wasters: *Thieves of Darkness,* Bk 2
https://a.co/d/bUvI9Jo

What Have You to Declare? What Do You Have With You from Where You've Been?

When I Was A Child, *I Prayed As a Child*

When the Devourer is Rebuked
https://a.co/d/1HVv8oq

When The Table Is Set Against You

WTH? Get Me Out of This Hell
https://a.co/d/a7WBGJh

The Wilderness Romance *(series)* This series is about conducting a Godly relationship and marriage with someone who is a Wilderness person. *The Social Wilderness*

- *The Sexual Wilderness*
- *The Spiritual Wilderness*

Other Series

The Fold (a series on Godly finances)

https://a.co/d/4hz3unj

Soul Prosperity Series https://a.co/d/bz2M42q

Spirit Spouse books

https://a.co/d/9VehDSo

https://a.co/d/97sKOwm

Battlefield of Marriage, The https://a.co/d/eUDzizO

Players Gonna Play

https://a.co/d/2hzGw3N

Sent Spirit Spouse (can someone send you a spirit spouse? This book is not yet released.)

Thieves of Darkness series

The Emptiers https://a.co/d/heioOdO

The Wasters https://a.co/d/5TG1iNQ

The Swallowers https://a.co/d/1jWhM6G

The Devourers: Why We Can't Have Nice Things https://a.co/d/87Tejbf

Dr. Marlene Miles is a teacher, author, and spiritual thinker known for her grounded, discerning approach to prayer and spiritual formation. Her work emphasizes clarity, restraint, and maturity in faith—helping believers move beyond emotionalism and performance into a steady, practiced walk with God.

With a deep respect for Scripture and a practical understanding of daily life, Dr. Miles writes for those who want their prayer life to be formed, not dramatized. Her teaching encourages spiritual maintenance, discernment, and responsibility—so faith remains strong not only in crisis, but in everyday living.

www.ingramcontent.com/pod-product-compliance
Lightning Source LLC
LaVergne TN
LVHW010704110826
845149LV00014B/3225

* 9 7 8 1 9 7 1 9 3 3 4 3 6 *